MW01049330

A Collection of Inspired Recipes,
Memories and Timeless Photographs

PEACHES & PAST TIMES
COOKBOOK

Collected by Lee Totzke

P AND P PUBLISHING
TEMPLE TEXAS

First Printing: 2008

ISBN: 978-0-9760462-2-6

For additional copies, send $24.95, plus $4.00 shipping (Texas residents add $1.97 sales tax) to:

P and P Publishing
3802 Antelope Trail
Temple TX 76504

Order on line: www.pandppublishing.com

For online press release and cover image, send request to: mkttx2@hot.rr.com

Cover and book design by Barbara Jezek, Austin, Texas

Printed in China

Buyers standing on truck looking at peach load, Benton Harbor Fruit Market 1938. Photo courtesy The Herald-Palladium, St. Joseph, Michigan.

Opposite: 4-H and F.F.A. Postage Pins created by Susan Miller, Miller Studio, Artist. Reproduced with permission.

Dedicated to American Peach Growers and their local, state, and national associations, and County Extension Service. To 4-H and leaders like Virginia Radewald who served 4-H and youth for over 60 years. For Agriculture and F.F.A. teachers like the Reverend Bill Wilson who are dedicated to youth and to their community.

As I view this empty garden bench where my Grandma Augusta Totzke and I used to sit and talk, it brings back memories of Grandma clipping sprigs of herbs, such as rosemary, to include with letters she was writing as remembrance. She would sit on the bench and write recipes to share with friends and family and I would get to the lick the envelopes.

CONTENTS

Slowhaul—1930 Chabbotts, Riverside, Michigan. Photo courtesy The Herald–Palladium, St. Joseph, Michigan.

ACKNOWLEDGEMENTS

I owe more thanks than I can possibly enumerate. While conducting interviews, I found myself trailing through peach orchards, having the lore of the land shared with enthusiastic smiles and at times with gut wrenching pain. The farmers opened their homes and hearts to me, fed me, shared old recipes and entrusted me with vintage documents, pictures, and heartfelt stories. I am deeply grateful to the people I have listed and ask forgiveness from those whose names I have overlooked.

Particular thanks goes to my publishers, Newman Marketing. Merikay and Jerry Jones continually encouraged me, from the first concept to the final draft with their humor and professional advice and editing.

My graphic designer, Barbara Jezek for making it beautiful and for making it happen.

To Doris Pesko for all the photographic reproductions and honest opinions.

With the love and endless hours given to our business by Donnie Minyard, while I was writing, this book would not have been a reality and I would still be eating cherries.

A special thank you to the hundreds of friends who sent me recipes. Some came from housewives, some from chefs in 4 and 5 star restaurants. We did not want to have duplicates and that was our criteria for eliminating some of the contributions.

Lee Totzke
February, 2008

PREFACE

Peaches and Past Times Cookbook started as a small project, a tribute to the Southwest Michigan peach growers of which my family played a part.

The word spread and peach growers in other parts of the U.S. wanted their story told. I have thoroughly enjoyed the two years of interviews. One interview started by phone and concluded with me driving over a thousand miles. I needed to look this person in the eyes! Another started at a dining room table and ended hours later in the attic, while we went through stained cardboard boxes that had not been opened in years and that contained farm journals and photographs, each telling a story.

Some recipes came from old well loved and rusted metal recipe boxes, including my mother's. The range of recipes varies from simple farm fare for large families with big appetites, to those more challenging creations from chefs in fine city cafes and restaurants. Pastry chefs are adding more peach delicacies to their repertoires.

Peach lovers and creative cooks are both sophisticated and knowledgeable, approaching their confections with an understanding of the varieties, white or yellow flesh, and the effect weather conditions present. Peaches are a topic for today much like wine, cigars and coffee. Each recipe is different and each will transport you to a different culinary destination.

Meeting with the original growers' grandchildren, great grandchildren and great-great-grandchildren who now operate some of family farms has been a pure joy. The phrase I heard repeatedly was "I love coming to work each day." Many have cultivated a devoted customer base and loyal employees. The best part of the journey for many has been the introduction of new varieties, so their picking season has been extended.

The black and white photographs take us back to the 1800's, while the color photographs bring us into the 21st century. The recipes follow the same time line.

The one definitive difference between this cookbook and the thousands of others on the market today is the collection of interviews, which make the stories and recipes so personal. I met children who have prepared nearly their entire life for their career as a grower. Immigrants expressed a passion for finding the American dream. I heard from growers who thought that they had lost it all, but who dug in and worked without pay to reinvent their farms so their lineage would carry on.

Although my name is normally associated with the Biblical Wreath I created, copyrighted and patented, I was born into a family of southwest Michigan fruit growers. Twelve miles from our farms was the Benton Harbor Fruit Market, which grew to be the largest wholesale grower-to-buyer fresh fruit market in the United States. This market organized in the late 1800's and continues today.

Berrien County, Michigan on Lake Michigan had the perfect growing conditions for orchards and vineyards. The same criteria along with the lake and rail for shipping found entrepreneur nurserymen moving to the area. Many of them today are still recognized as great fruit tree breeders of their time. They not only sold locally, but as the West was settled it, too became a major buyer of fruit trees, as was Texas.

I hope you enjoy your journey — it has been a wonderful one for me and my family and my friends — both new ones and treasured people who have helped me along the way.

THE PEACH

First recorded in 2000 B.C. China, the peach was formerly believed to have come from Persia, explaining its scientific name (prunus persica), although there are no records to prove this theory. It was brought to Europe before the first century B.C., probably by Alexander the Great. In the 16th century, the Spanish took the peach to South America and by the 17th century, it was growing in the U.S.A.

Today the Chinese use peach blossoms to decorate their homes at New Years to signify spring. This custom began with the early Chinese who used peach blossoms to ward off ill health and evil. As an example, parents would place necklaces made from peach pips on their children to drive away demons. The tree continues to represent marriage, good fortune, youth and long life.

In March, during the Girls' Festival in Japan, branches of peach blossoms are used to decorate and inspire thoughts of immortality, feminine charm and marriage. The peach also represents fertility, while the branches are used as divining rods. Numerous fruits were used in Christian symbolism: the peach represents the fruit of salvation and virtue. Those who ate the fruit were said to be given wisdom. In Culpeper's early Herbal he said it provoked lust.

For centuries, the peach has been used for culinary and medicinal parts. The kernels, which are filled with prussic acid like almonds, should not be eaten in excess. First Century physician Dioscorides recommended they be eaten in moderation to benefit digestion and a 2nd Century physician recorded that it stimulated the appetite.

A tincture of peach flowers was used to relieve colic caused by kidney stones and gravel. Later in the summer the herb Nigella flower was used to relieve colic. A syrup and infusion of peach flowers was given to weak children and used to treat jaundice. Culpeper said "the leaves laid on the belly killed worms and when powdered and strewn on fresh bleeding wounds stayeth their bleeding and closeth them." In his early Herbal, which is still used by scholars today, he recommends for the cure of migraine to apply the milk of the kernels and the oil expressed from them to the forehead.

Today in the U.S., one out of three hundred people receive their primary heath care from plants. In other parts of the world, it is one out of three people. An example of that is the peach, which has fallen in medicinal use. The fruit is still enjoyed and has a wealth of health benefits.

Like many other fruits, those benefits are contained in the peel. The peach is a good source of vitamin C and other vitamins and minerals, and especially when dried, are a good source of iron and potassium. Digested easily, it is both a mild laxative and a gentle diuretic, aiding elimination of toxins and relieving fluid retention. The juice will sooth an irritated urinary system and has a calming effect on the nervous system. Some have said it helps to lower blood cholesterol. Ladies used to crush peaches and apply them to the face each day as a beauty aid to keep the skin cool and young looking. Aveda, one of our leading hair and beauty aid companies, continues to use a part of the peach in their hair conditioner.

Appetizers & Beverages

PEACH PROSCIUTTO

- ¼ cup lime juice
- 8 South Carolina peaches sliced into 6 pieces—Do Not Peel
- 9 ounces thinly sliced prosciutto (a thinly sliced Italian ham)
- 36 sprigs fresh mint

Place peach slices into a bowl, and sprinkle with lime juice. Stir gently to coat. Wrap each slice with a strip of prosciutto, and secure with a sprig of mint. Arrange on a serving tray. Refrigerate until serving.

Courtesy of South Carolina Peach Council

MOLTEN GOLDEN BRIE WITH FRESH SOUTH CAROLINA PEACHES

- 1 fresh South Carolina peach, pitted and thinly sliced
- 1 fresh lemon
- 1 (1 pound) wheel of Brie cheese
- 1 bottle Molten Golden hot sauce
- ¼ cup brown sugar
- ½ cup sliced almonds

Heat oven to 325 degrees. Slice the peach into thin slices. Squeeze fresh lemon juice over peach slices and set aside. Place Brie cheese on a baking sheet and cover with a generous layer of Molten Golden. Sprinkle with brown sugar, and then top with peach slices in a single layer. Bake for 10 minutes and remove from oven. Add sliced almonds and continue baking until almonds are toasted. Serve with crackers.

©Palmetto Pepper Potions • Molten Golden hot sauce is a product of Palmetto Pepper Potions. www.pepperpotions.com. Published by South Carolina Peach Council

FRUITED KABOBS

6 *medium peaches*
1 *quart fresh blueberries*
4 *large bananas*
1 *cup plain yogurt*
1 *pint any fruit juice*
1 *tablespoon grated lemon rind*
1 *cup marshmallow cream*
1 *quart fresh strawberries*

Wash and slice peaches. Slice banana into ½-inch rounds. Place sliced fruit into fruit juice for 5 minutes. Drain well. Wash strawberries and blueberries. Thread fruit onto 12 (8-inch) bamboo skewers. Chill. Combine remaining ingredients. Mix well. Serve as a sauce with fruit kabobs. Makes 12 kabobs.

Courtesy of South Carolina Department of Agriculture

GRILLED STONE FRUIT

4 *tablespoons unsalted butter, melted*
½ *teaspoon pure vanilla extract*
2 *peaches, pitted and halved*
2 *nectarines, pitted and halved*
2 *plums pitted and halved*
1 *tablespoon sugar*
1 *bunch fresh mint for garnish*
Vanilla ice cream (optional)

Preheat a well oiled grill to medium. Combine the melted butter and vanilla extract and lightly brush over the cut sides of fruit. Place fruit on a plate and sprinkle lightly with sugar. Place fruit, cut side down, on grill for EXACTLY four minutes. Carefully remove to a serving plate with a spatula and arrange decoratively. Garnish with a big bunch of mint in the center of the platter and serve with ice cream, if desired. Serves 6.

Courtesy of Abbott Fruit Markets and South Carolina Peach Council

FUZZY ALMOND

1 ounce peach schnapps
1 ounce Amaretto

Shake with ice. Strain into a chilled glass over ice. Garnish with a small slice of orange.

Courtesy of South Carolina Peach Council

PEACH SANGRIA

Even people who don't like red wine will think this drink is peachy keen!

4 (750 milliliter) bottles red wine
1¼ cups white sugar or measured sugar substitute equivalent
2 Granny Smith apples, peeled, cored and sliced
4 sliced fresh South Carolina peaches
2 bananas, peeled and sliced
2 cinnamon sticks, crushed
3 liters lemon-lime flavored (regular or diet) carbonated beverage

In a large pitcher, combine red wine, sugar, apples, peaches, bananas and cinnamon sticks. Refrigerate for 6 hours or overnight. When you're ready to serve, stir in the lemon-lime soda. Serves 48.

Courtesy of South Carolina Peach Council

PEACH LEMON SANGRIA

1 cup fresh lemon juice (about 5 lemons)
2 quarts cold water
4 tablespoons sugar
1 cup peach slices
16 mint leaves

Blend lemon juice, water and gradually add sugar while stirring. Refrigerate for 2 hours. Peel, pit and slice ripe peaches into tall stem glasses and immediately pour liquid over peaches. Garnish with mint leaves. Serves 8.

SERIOUS STRESS RELIEVER

1 ounce vodka
1 ounce dark rum
1 ounce peach schnapps
1 ounce orange juice
1 ounce cranberry juice
1 South Carolina peach slice

In a cocktail shaker, combine vodka, rum, peach schnapps, orange juice and cranberry juice. Shake well. Pour over ice in a tall glass and garnish with the peach slice.

Courtesy of South Carolina Peach Council

LUIS SANDOVAL

*"I only ask God for two things —
health and work."*

Luis Sandoval, a native of Mexico, at age 20
moved to Chicago on a hot September day
in 1973. The following summer he became a
migrant laborer across Lake Michigan on the
Nye Farms south of St. Joseph, Michigan. He
would return to Chicago in the winter to work
in a factory as a welder. He decided he wanted
to stay in the U.S. so he applied for his green
card. In 1976, Luis, his pregnant wife and their
little girl moved to Texas near Houston where
Luis found year round work as a metal worker.
In 1982 he was laid off from work so he joined
a program to become a certified welder.
He worked for a welder for a few years but his
real love remained working in the orchards. He
decided to return to Nye Farms in the
summer of 1983 and continued each summer
until 1988 when Luis asked Mr. Nye for a year
round position and Mr. Nye agreed to hire
him. Luis also decided to become an American
citizen and that was one of the happiest days
of his life. Mr. Nye recognized Luis potential
and continued to give him more management
responsibilities involving the daily operations of
the farm. In 1995, Gordon Nye turned over the

continued on page 16

complete operation of the farm to Luis and from that date, Luis gradually bought Nye Farms.

Our interview took place on the steps of a small house in the midst of a fully blooming fruit orchard. I always knew the house as "grandma's house" when I was growing up. It was where Mrs. Nye's mother lived. As we stood and talked, the scent of apple and peach blossoms filled the air. I could see in Luis's eyes how proud he was of his farm, as he continued to speak of his family. Three of his daughters joined the armed forces. One was in the Navy, another in the Army and the third in the Air Force. One daughter has gone on to become a recruiter. The two younger children are still in school and work on the farm. Their father had just planted 900 more Baby Gold trees, which Gerber Baby food uses. His primary buyers are Amish communities in Mississippi and Kentucky. I asked Luis if he would have a Spanish recipe to share with me and he said "No. Recipes take time to make and we don't have the time so we eat all the fresh peaches we can during the season." Luis truly feels he has been blessed and he says: "I only ask God for two things – health and work."

PEACH DAIQUIRI

- ½ medium unpeeled ripe peach, cut into chunks
- 1½ ounces white rum
- ½ ounce fresh lime juice
- 2 teaspoons sugar
- ¾ cup crushed ice

Place all ingredients into a blender, cover and process for 10 seconds at high speed. Chill two stemmed glasses and fill with daiquiri mixture. Garnish with a lime slice and a peach slice.

FROZEN PEACH DAIQUIRIS

- 2½ ounces dark rum
- ¼ cup freshly squeezed lime juice
- ¼ cup sugar
- 9 peach ice cubes (see recipe below)
- ¾ cup crushed ice

Combine all ingredients in a blender; blend smooth. Pour into stemmed glasses. Garnish with peach and lime slices. Makes three 6-ounce drinks.
*For non-alcoholic version, substitute pineapple juice for rum and decrease sugar to two tablespoons.

PEACH ICE CUBES

Good served in sweet tea or rum.

4 fresh peaches, peeled and sliced
1 tablespoon lemon juice

Combine in blender, puree. Pour into ice cube trays; freeze.

Courtesy of Big Smile Peaches of J.W. Yonce & Sons, Inc. Published by South Carolina Peach Council

PEACH MELBA SMOOTHIE

4 South Carolina Peaches, peeled and sliced
1 (8-ounce) container raspberry fat-free yogurt
1 (8-ounce) container peach fat-free yogurt
1 cup skim milk
8 ice cubes
¼ cup raspberries

Reserve 4 peach slices and 8 berries for garnish. In a blender, blend all ingredients. Pour into tall, chilled glasses. Garnish with reserved peach slices and raspberries.

Courtesy of South Carolina Peach Council

PERSONALLY FIT PEACH MORNING SMOOTHIE

3 South Carolina peaches, peeled and sliced
1 medium banana
1½ cups skim milk
1 cup lemon or vanilla fat free yogurt
2 tablespoons honey
1 package cinnamon spice instant oatmeal

Puree all ingredients in a blender until smooth. Blend with ice if preferred. Serve in chilled glasses. Serves 4.

Created for the South Carolina Peach Council by Matt Fulmer, owner of Personally Fit, Columbia, SC.

PEACHY-PINEAPPLE SMOOTHIE

28 ounces sliced peaches
½ cup pineapple juice, chilled
¼ cup sugar
1 pint vanilla ice cream, softened

Process first 3 ingredients in a blender until smooth, stopping once to scrape down sides. Add ice cream; process until smooth and serve immediately.

LOW CAL PEACH FROSTY

1 (8.5-ounce) can unsweetened, sliced peaches, drained
2 cups unsweetened orange juice
1 pint vanilla ice milk
¼ cup plain yogurt
⅛ teaspoon ground cinnamon
⅛ teaspoon ground nutmeg

Place all ingredients in a blender. Process until smooth. Serve immediately. Makes 5 cups.

Thanks to Bettye J. Knott, Waxahachie, Texas

FRESH PEACH SHAKE

½ teaspoon lemon juice
½ teaspoon ground cardamom
2 tablespoons granulated sugar
1 cup ice cubes
1 cup sliced ripe peaches
Pinch of salt
2 cups whole milk yogurt

Drizzle lemon juice over sliced peaches, gently stir. Pour peaches in blender along with other ingredients. Blend until mixture is smooth. Pour into shake glasses and serve.

PEACH SHAKE

1 cup diced ripe peaches
1½ tablespoons sugar
2 tablespoons lemon juice
1 cup cold milk
½ pint vanilla ice cream

Mix well until thick and fluffy. Serves 2.

PEACH NOG

3 chilled South Carolina peaches, peeled and sliced
1 cup cold skim milk
1 teaspoon lemon juice

In a blender, mix peaches, skim milk and lemon juice until smooth. Serve immediately. For thicker drink, freeze sliced peaches first. Serves 1.

Courtesy of YMCA of Uptown Columbia. Published by South Carolina Peach Council

PEACH JUICE

- ¾ cup sugar
- 4 strips lemon zest
- 2¼ cups water
- 1 ripe nectarine
- 4 pounds ripe South Carolina peaches, peeled, halved, pitted, and cut into chunks

Juice of 1 lemon

Cold sparkling wine or club soda (optional)

Bring sugar, zest, and water to a boil in a medium pot, stirring to dissolve sugar. Cook until a syrup forms, about 5 minutes. Reduce to a simmer. Add nectarine; cook until syrup turns pink, about 3 minutes. Using a slotted spoon, transfer nectarine to a plate to cool. Transfer syrup to an airtight container; refrigerate about 1 hour. Peel nectarine, and cut it into large chunks; discard pit. Transfer nectarine to a large bowl. Add peaches and lemon juice to bowl. Using your hands or a potato masher, mash to extract as much juice as possible. Lightly press through a sieve into another bowl; discard solids. Stir in cooled syrup. Juice can be refrigerated up to 3 days. Serve over ice with sparkling wine or club soda if desired. Makes about 1 quart.

Courtesy of South Carolina Peach Council

PEACH LEMONADE

- 5 lemons, squeeze 1 cup juice
- 2 quarts cold water
- 4 tablespoons granulated sugar
- 1 cup ripe peach slices
- 16 mint leaves, reserve

Blend four top ingredients until smooth. Pour in glasses over ice. Serve with a straw and garnish each glass with mint leaves.

GEORGIA PEACH ICED TEA

3 (11½-ounce) cans Georgia peach nectar
1 cup sugar
2 quarts brewed tea
¼ cup fresh lemon juice

Stir together all ingredients; chill until ready to serve. Yield: ¾ gallon.

Courtesy of Dickey Farms, Musella, Georgia, "The Sweetest Peaches in the South"

PEACH TEA MIX

Great Gift Idea!

1 cup instant tea mix
1 (3-ounce) package peach gelatin
2 cups sugar

DRY MIX DIRECTIONS:

Combine all ingredients into an attractive container such as a clean jam or pickle jar. Seal tightly. Tie a decorative ribbon around the top of the container. Write the following directions for one serving of peach tea onto an attractive recipe card. Attach directions to container with another ribbon and tie into a bow.

If preparing for your own personal use, this is easily mixed and stored in a Ziploc® bag or plastic container.

DIRECTIONS FOR 1 SERVING OF PEACH TEA:

Combine 1 heaping tablespoon of tea mix with 6 ounces hot water. Allow to cool and serve with ice. Garnish with a slice of fresh peach.

Courtesy of South Carolina Peach Council

Employees on the Paul Friday Farm thin peaches in early spring.

(Opposite) George Friday, vetetan grower, tells late buyers the load is sold as he puts the sale ticket in his shirt pocket. Benton Harbor Fruit Market, Labor Day Weekend 1954. Courtesy The Herald–Palladium St. Joseph, Michigan.

Lane Packing Company

Lane Packing Company, Fort Valley, Georgia, is a fourth generation family operation that farms over 2,500 acres of peach trees and 2,000 acres of pecans. Located off I-75 in the middle of Georgia two hours from Atlanta. They participate in the H2A program and employ 400-500.

Lane Packing Company has the largest state of the art peach packing facility in Georgia. Customers are encouraged to use the elevated cat walk to view the packing process. I was impressed by the "Georgia Peach Basket". This unique basket, shaped like the state of Georgia, is filled with a wide selection of "peachy products".

Besides over 30 varieties of peaches, the current owners Duke Lane Jr., Bobby Lane, Steve Lane, and Anne Lane Tribble are adding to their growth by introducing citrus to their line of quality products. With the fifth generation involved in the daily work schedule it helps to assure the continued growth of Lane Packing Company.

Farm Receipts for Month of _____
Date

Farm Expenditures for Month of _____
Date

HARALSON
THE BIG RED WINTER
See Page 31

OPATA PLUM
See Page 31

SAPA P
See Pag

CHIEF
EARLIEST
RASPBERRY

GEORGIA PEACHES
STAR
BRAND

THIS CRATE
CONTAINS
6 FOUR QUART
BASKETS

GROWN & PACKED BY
W. J. BRADDY
WOODLAND, GEORGIA

PEACH PUNCH

- 2 cups Canada Dry Soda
- 1 (46-ounce) can unsweetened pineapple juice, refrigerated
- 1 (46-ounce) can peach nectar, refrigerated
- 3 (750 mil) bottles champagne, refrigerated

Combine soda, juice and nectar in a large, chilled punch bowl. Add champagne, stirring slowly. Garnish with red raspberries and orange slices.

FRUIT JUICY RUM PUNCH

- 2 cups orange juice
- 2 cups lemonade drink
- 1 (6-ounce) can frozen orange juice
- 1 (6-ounce) can frozen lemonade
- ½ cup sugar
- 1½ cups light rum or Malibu Rum
- 7 cups chilled ginger ale (optional)

Combine orange juice, lemonade drink, frozen juices, sugar and rum. Freeze 8 hours. Before serving, let punch stand at room temperature for at least 20 minutes. If desired, add chilled ginger ale.

Thanks to Brooksie Malone, Waxahachie, Texas

PEACH TEA PUNCH

- 4 cups water
- 3 family-size tea bags
- 2 cups loosely packed fresh mint leaves
- 1 (33.8-ounce) bottle peach nectar
- 1 (6-ounce) can frozen lemonade concentrate, thawed
- ½ cup Simple Sugar Syrup*
- 1 (1-liter) bottle ginger ale, chilled
- 1 (1-liter) bottle club soda, chilled

Mint sprigs

Bring 4 cups water to a boil in a medium saucepan; add tea bags and 2 cups mint leaves. Boil 1 minute; remove from heat. Cover and steep 10 minutes. Remove and discard tea bags and mint. Pour into a 1-gallon container; add peach nectar, lemonade concentrate, and Simple Sugar Syrup. Cover and chill 8 hours or overnight. Pour chilled tea mixture into a punch bowl. Stir in ginger ale and club soda just before serving. Garnish with fresh mint. Makes 1 gallon.

*SIMPLE SUGAR SYRUP

- 2 cups sugar
- 1 cup water

Bring sugar and water to boil in a medium saucepan over medium-high heat. Boil, stirring constantly, 4 minutes or until sugar dissolved and mixture is clear. Cool to room temperature. Makes 2½ cups.

Courtesy of South Carolina Peach Council

Soups, Salads, & Side Dishes

PEACH SALSA I

Makes a good complement to steaks or pork chops.

    4 ripe firm peaches, peeled and chopped
    1 cup chopped green onions
    ½ teaspoon crushed red pepper flakes
    ½ teaspoon salt
    ¼ teaspoon white pepper
    2 tablespoons chopped cilantro
    2 tablespoons lime juice
    ¼ cup finely chopped yellow bell pepper
    ¼ cup finely chopped orange bell pepper

In chilled non-metal bowl, gently stir together all ingredients and cover. Refrigerate for 90 minutes before serving.

PEACH SALSA II

    8 ripe Michigan peaches
    ½ cup chopped red onion
    ½ cup chopped yellow or orange bell pepper
    ¼ cup chopped fresh cilantro
    3 limes

Cut peaches into small pieces. Mince onion and bell pepper. Chop fresh cilantro. Toss all ingredients with juice of all three limes. This not only adds great flavor, it adds a palate of color to fish or meat on the grill.

GEORGIA PEACH-AVOCADO SALSA

    2 large fresh Georgia peaches, peeled
       and diced
    1 tablespoon lime juice
    ¼ cup diced jicama (optional)
    1 teaspoon olive oil
    2 Roma tomatoes, seeded and diced
    ¼ teaspoon salt
    1 small avocado, diced
    ¼ teaspoon ground red pepper
    1 tablespoon minced red onion

Combine all ingredients in a large bowl. Cover and chill until ready to serve. Yield: 2¾ cups.

Courtesy of Dickey Farms, Musella, Georgia, "The Sweetest Peaches in the South"

PEACH WHIP DIP

    1 cup frozen whipped topping
    1 cup peach yogurt
    ½ cup finely chopped peaches

Mix whipped topping, yogurt and chopped peaches. Chill. Serve with fresh fruit. Makes 2 cups.

Courtesy of Sharon McFall, Busy Woman's Cookbook©

(Opposite upper right) Big sister says you have to go out to the orchard with us.

PEACH SALSA III

2 cups peeled, sliced South Carolina peaches

2 cups diced cantaloupe

1 pint strawberries, hulled, sliced

2 Roma tomatoes, diced

1 cup diced red onion

1 large jalapeño, seeded, diced

¼ cup cilantro, chopped, do not pack in measuring cup

Salt and pepper to taste

6 tablespoons lime juice

1 tablespoon extra virgin olive oil

Combine all the chopped ingredients in a large bowl. Gently stir. Season with salt and pepper. Add lime juice and oil. Let sit for 15 minutes. Serves 8.

Courtesy of South Carolina Peach Council

HEAVENLY SOUP

3 *South Carolina peaches, peeled and sliced*
1 *teaspoon lemon juice*
1 *tablespoon sugar*
2 *tablespoons butter*
1½ *tablespoons flour*
¼ *teaspoon salt*
1 *cup half and half*
Sour cream, if desired

In a blender, puree peaches and measure off 1¼ cups puree. Save any remaining puree for a later use. Mix in sugar and lemon juice. Melt butter in medium size sauce pan. Mix in flour and salt; heat until bubbly. Add the half and half and puree mixture. Cook over low to moderate heat, stirring constantly, until thick. Serve warm or cold. Garnish with a dollop of sour cream. Soup can be made a day ahead of time and stored in refrigerator. Serves 4.

Courtesy of South Carolina Peach Council

CHILLED MELON, PAPAYA AND PEACH SOUP

2 *large ripe cantaloupes, peeled, seeded and chopped*
1 *ripe papaya, peeled, seeded and chopped*
2 *South Carolina peaches, cut up and pitted*
⅓ *cup non fat plain yogurt*
1 *tablespoon honey*
⅛ *teaspoon ground nutmeg*
Mint sprigs for garnish

Place papaya in food processor and process until smooth; add cantaloupe and process in batches until pureed; add peaches until pureed. Add yogurt, honey and nutmeg; process until mixture is smooth and well combined. Transfer soup to large bowl; cover and refrigerate until well chilled, about 1 hour. Serve soup in crystal bowls or wine glasses. Garnish with mint sprigs before serving. Serves 6–8.

Courtesy of South Carolina Peach Council

CHILLED GEORGIA PEACH SOUP

3 cardamom seeds*

3 whole cloves

2 pounds Georgia peaches, peeled and coarsely chopped

2 cups orange juice

3 tablespoons lime juice

¼ cup honey

1½ teaspoons ground cinnamon

1 teaspoon ground ginger

1 (8-ounce) container vanilla low-fat yogurt

1 teaspoon diced candied ginger

Place cardamom and cloves on a 6-inch square of cheesecloth; tie with string. Bring spice bag, chopped peaches, orange juice, and next 4 ingredients to a boil in a large saucepan. Reduce heat; simmer, stirring occasionally, 10 minutes or until peach is tender. Remove and discard spice bag; let peach mixture cool. Process peach mixture in batches in a blender or food processor until smooth; stir in yogurt and ginger. Cover and chill; garnish with fresh mint sprigs or peach slices if desired. Yield: 6 cups.

*⅛ teaspoon ground cardamom may be substituted; stir in with cinnamon and ginger.

Courtesy of Dickey Farms, Musella, Georgia, "The Sweetest Peaches in the South"

Interior of packing house of J.K. Barden & Son, Casco, Michigan. Peach Picking (below), J.C. Johnston, Kibbie, Michigan. Photos Courtesy Dr. Paul Rood and the State Horticultural Society of Michigan.

Dickey Farms is home to Georgia's oldest, continuously operating peach packinghouse. Built in 1936 from lumber hewn off the land of Robert L. "Mr. Bob" Dickey, the long, white building is a prominent landmark in Musella, Georgia. At the time of construction, the packinghouse was ideally located near rail lines for better transportation to the peach-hungry North.

"Mr. Bob" was an early pioneer of "multi-tasking", being a postmaster, undertaker, depot agent and general store manager. However, his heart was in the peach industry, and we are reaping the rewards today.

In the early days of Dickey Farms mules were used to plow the orchards and also for transportation of peaches to the packinghouse. At that time, most of the work was done manually. However, "Mr. Bob" was a forward-thinker, always wanting to introduce labor saving equipment. He installed Georgia's very first brushing machine to remove the peach fuzz. He was also one of the first producers to include a hydro-cooling system that places peaches in 35-degree water to remove field dust and slow the ripening process, making them perfect when reaching the northern markets.

Today, his grandson, Robert L. Dickey, II and his great-grandson, Robert L. Dickey, III, work together to ensure that a Dickey Farms peach is the freshest, most succulent fruit available. While "Mr. Bob" shipped all his fruit by refrigerated railroad cars, peaches today are shipped by refrigerated trucks, which can reach some markets overnight. Although many changes in the industry have been made over the last 100 years, the Dickey family still continues the tradition of providing the highest quality peach.

http://www.gapeaches.com/index.htm

SALUDA COUNTY PEACH GAZPACHO

2 cups peeled, pitted and diced South Carolina peaches (about 1.5 pounds)

1 large red tomato, diced

1 medium yellow tomato, diced

1 seedless cucumber, unpeeled, diced

½ cup green bell pepper, diced

3 tablespoons chopped fresh cilantro

2 tablespoons fresh lime juice

1 tablespoon fresh minced garlic

2 teaspoons minced jalapeno

4 cups V-8 juice (32-ounces)

1 teaspoon toasted black and white sesame seeds

1 teaspoon sugar

½ teaspoon cumin

Salt and pepper to taste

Place ingredients in order listed in large mixing bowl. Stir to blend ingredients, cover and place in refrigerator for at least 1 hour before serving. Serve in chilled soup bowls.

Recipe complements of Brandon Velie, Chef/Owner of Juniper, Ridge Spring, SC and Executive Chef of The Green Boundary Club Aiken, SC. Published by South Carolina Peach Council.

PEACHY SOUTHERN SLAW

1 cup pecan pieces

1 head savoy cabbage, sliced

8 fresh South Carolina peaches, pitted and
   sliced

1 red bell pepper, sliced

1 yellow bell pepper, sliced

½ cup chopped green onions

2 tablespoons celery seed

DRESSING

½ cup fresh South Carolina peaches, pitted
   and chopped

½ cup vegetable oil

¼ cup honey

¼ cup lemon juice

Salt and pepper to taste

1 bunch fresh mint sprigs

Place the pecan pieces in a skillet over medium heat, and cook, stirring constantly, until lightly toasted. In a large bowl, mix the pecans, cabbage, 8 fresh peaches, red bell pepper, yellow bell pepper, green onions, and celery seed. Cover and chill 45 minutes in the refrigerator.

Dressing: In a blender or food processor, blend the ½ cup chopped peaches until smooth. Transfer to a bowl, and mix with the oil, honey, lemon juice, salt, and pepper. Chill until slaw is ready to be served, toss with slaw to coat. Garnish slaw with mint sprigs.

Courtesy of South Carolina Peach Council

FRIED PEACH HALVES

8 cooked peach halves
2 cups cereal flakes, corn or bran
Crisco for pan frying

Roll peach halves in cereal flakes.
Pan fry lightly in Crisco. Serve
as an accompainment to meat.
Serves 8.

PEACH BEET SALAD

2 (5-ounce) packages spring mix salad
   greens
2 cups sliced fresh peaches
1 can (13¼ ounce) sliced beets, drained
½ cup balsamic vinaigrette
½ cup crumbled feta cheese

In a large salad bowl, combine greens, peach slices and beets. Drizzle with dressing and toss gently to coat. Sprinkle with feta cheese and serve. Serves 8.

Courtesy of South Carolina Peach Council

PEACHES WITH FRESH SALAD AND CHEESE

Complement with a glass of white Merlot

4 large ripe peaches
1 cup fresh mint leaves
¼ cup granulated or raw sugar
2 tablespoons balsamic vinegar
1 teaspoon lemon juice
⅛ teaspoon fresh ground black pepper
2 tablespoons chopped almonds, toasted
8 cups fresh salad greens
1 (6-ounce) round Brie cheese, cut into 8
   wedges or sharp Vermont Cheddar
8 slices French bread

Fill a large saucepan half full with water. Bring to a full boil and place peaches in water for 30 seconds, remove and immediately place in ice water. Remove loose skins by hand or with a paring knife. Cut each peach in half and remove stone.

Place fresh mint and raw sugar in a food processor and pulse. Combine balsamic vinegar and fresh ground pepper; continue to pulse until blended. Pour mixture into a large chilled bowl; add toasted almonds and peaches. Drizzle lemon juice over peaches. Cover and refrigerate for 4 to 6 hours. Use a slotted spoon to remove peach halves; reserve dressing.

Prepare 1 cup of field greens on 8 salad plates, placing peach half on each mound of greens, a wedge of cheese and slice of bread. Drizzle dressing over peach half and greens.

CARROT, FRUIT, AND SPINACH SALAD

2　medium carrots, peeled, cut lengthwise into thin strips

1½　cups fresh or canned pineapple chunks, drained

¼　cup raisins

¼　cup pecan pieces

½　cup plain low-fat yogurt

1　(16-ounce) can orange juice concentrate, thawed

1　medium yellow peach, sliced

1½　cups torn spinach

In a bowl, combine carrots, pineapple, raisin and pecan pieces. Stir together yogurt and orange juice concentrate. Stir yogurt dressing into carrot mixture. Cover and chill 4 hours or up to 3 days. Cut peaches into slices and toss with carrot salad. Serve on plates lined with spinach leaves.

Thanks to Bettye J. Knott, Waxahachie, Texas

LADYBUG SALAD

2　peaches

¼　cup raisins

½　cup peanut butter

4　lettuce leaves

8　thin pretzel sticks

24　red grapes

Slice peaches in half from top to bottom, and scoop out the pits. Spread 1 tablespoon peanut butter on the cut side of the peach. On 4 small plates, place one 1 lettuce leaf. Place peach, peanut butter side down, onto lettuce. Stick raisins onto peaches with the remaining peanut butter for spots. Use this method to make eyes too. Stick one end of 2 pretzels into the peach to make antennae. Arrange 3 grapes along each side of peach to make legs. Enjoy! Serves 4.

Courtesy of South Carolina Peach Council

LADYBUG SITTING ON A PEACH

Cool Whip® or spray whip crème
Halved pitted peaches
 Red grapes
Strawberries
Mini chocolate chips
Pretzel Sticks

For each one, spread a plate with Cool Whip® and top with a peach half. Push half of a red grape onto a toothpick for the head. Next, push onto the toothpick a hulled strawberry body and score the back to create wings. For spots, use another toothpick to gently press mini chocolate chips, tips down, into the side with the wings. For antennae, break one pretzel stick in half. Stick the broken ends into the berry at the base of the grape head. Take a trimmed wooden skewer and stick into the opposite side of the berry. Stick the skewer into the peach half and serve.

Courtesy of South Carolina Peach Council

PEACH WALDORF SALAD

 6 large South Carolina peaches
 1 cup diced celery
 1 cup chopped walnuts
 2 tablespoons honey
 ½ cup sour cream
 12 or more fresh strawberries
Salad greens

Peel and slice peaches. In a large bowl toss peaches, celery, nuts and honey. Chill well. At serving time, fold in sour cream and pile on lettuce leaves on salad plates. Garnish with whole strawberries.

Courtesy of South Carolina Peach Council

BERRY BEST SALAD

Only 15 minutes preparation time from start to finish

- ¼ cup orange juice
- 1 tablespoon salad oil
- 2 teaspoons honey mustard or Dijon
- 1 teaspoon sugar
- ¼ teaspoon salt
- 4 cups torn lettuce
- 1½ cups blueberries, fresh raspberries, strawberries
- ¼ canned mandarin orange sections, drained

Peach slices, canned or fresh

- ¼ cup Cheddar fish crackers or pretzels
- 1 tablespoon sunflower seed or pecans, shelled

Dressing: combine orange juice, oil, mustard, sugar and salt. Place ingredients in a jar and shake. Place lettuce in bowl, add fruit on top and drizzle with dressing. Serves 4.

Thanks to Bettye J. Knott, Waxahachie, Texas

Opposite: Poster (top) courtesy of Shafer Orchards, Baroda, Michigan. Bob Lausman Sr. (below) heads to market with his newly loaded Shafer Farms peaches.

PEACH TORTELLINI SALAD

- 1 (12-ounce) package refrigerated cheese-filled tortellini
- 3 cups sliced Georgia peaches
- 1 medium red bell pepper, cut into match sticks
- ¼ cup basil peach vinaigrette (more to taste) (see recipe below)
- 4 cups mixed fresh salad greens

Cook tortellini according to package directions. Rinse until cool; drain well. In medium bowl, combine tortellini, peaches and red pepper. Chill until ready to serve. Drizzle vinaigrette over mixture, toss gently. Place salad greens on large serving platter or use 4 individual salad plates. Arrange peach tortellini mixture over greens. Yield: 4 servings.

BASIL PEACH VINAIGRETTE

- ½ cup peach preserves
- ¼ cup peach vinegar
- ½ teaspoon seasoning salt
- ½ teaspoon Italian seasoning
- ½ teaspoon finely chopped fresh basil
- ½ cup olive oil

Combine all ingredients in the food processor bowl; process until smooth. Refrigerate until ready to use.

Georgia Department of Agriculture

CHEESE AND PEACH SANDWICHES

- 1 (8-ounce) package light cream cheese
- 1 cup chopped walnuts
- 1 cup chopped dates
- 6 South Carolina Peaches, peeled and sliced in half
- Romaine lettuce
- Strawberries
- Black olives

Soften cream cheese. In a medium bowl, mix the cream cheese, walnuts and dates together with a handheld beater. Put filling between 2 peach halves. Serve on lettuce with strawberries and black olives. Serves 6.

Courtesy of South Carolina Peach Council

PEACH CHEESE SALAD

- 8   halves ripe firm peaches
- ½   cup Neufchatel cheese
- ¼   cup French dressing
- 1   cup whipped cream, whipped until stiff peaks form
- ½   cup nut meats

Place a peach half on fresh lettuce. Make cheese into balls and fill centers of peaches. Mix French dressing with whipped cream. Put a portion on top of cheese, sprinkle with nuts. Serve.

A good form of spray rig for tall trees.
Photo Courtesy Dr. Paul Rood and the State
Horticultural Society of Michigan.

PEACHES AND CHEESE

- 2   cups small curd cottage cheese, drained
- 4   tablespoons coarsely chopped walnuts
- 4   tablespoons Hellman's® mayonnaise
- ¼   teaspoon ground nutmeg
- 1   head of leaf lettuce
- 8   ripe firm peach halves
- 2   cups sliced strawberries

In a large, chilled mixing bowl, combine cottage cheese, walnuts, mayonnaise, and nutmeg. On 8 salad plates, place one leaf of lettuce, layered with a peach half and strawberries arranged around it. Carefully cover the fruit with the cheese mixture.

QUICK TO FIX SPICED PEACHES

1 large can peach halves (free stone)
½ cup packed brown sugar
3 tablespoons margarine or butter
1 teaspoon cinnamon

Drain juice from peaches into a large saucepan. Add brown sugar, butter and cinnamon. Mix well. Add peaches and simmer for 15 minutes. Remove peaches from syrup using a slotted spoon. An excellent accompaniment to pork, doves or duck. Serves 4.

Thanks to Bettye J. Knott, Waxahachie, Texas

SPICED PEACHES

2 large cans peach halves
1⅓ cups sugar
1 cup cider vinegar
4 cinnamon sticks
3 teaspoons whole cloves

Drain peaches. Reserve syrup. Combine peach syrup, sugar, vinegar, cinnamon sticks and cloves in saucepan. Bring mixture to a boil, then lower heat and simmer 10 minutes. Pour hot syrup over peach halves. Let cool and chill thoroughly.

Thanks to Brooksie Malone, Waxahachie, Texas

GRILLED BALSAMIC-GLAZED GEORGIA PEACHES

½ cup balsamic vinegar
3 tablespoons brown sugar
1 teaspoon cracked pepper
⅛ teaspoon salt
6 firm, ripe Georgia peaches, halved
¼ cup vegetable oil

Combine first 4 ingredients in a saucepan. Bring to a boil; reduce heat, and simmer 2 to 3 minutes. Place peaches in a shallow dish. Pour vinegar mixture over peaches, tossing gently to coat. Let stand 10 minutes. Remove peaches from vinegar mixture, reserving 2 tablespoons mixture. Set aside remaining vinegar mixture. Whisk together reserved 2 tablespoons vinegar mixture and oil, blending well. Set vinaigrette aside. Place peach halves, cut sides down, on a lightly greased grill rack. Grill, covered with grill lid, over medium heat, 300–350 degrees, for 5 minutes on each side or until firm and golden, basting with remaining vinegar mixture. Serve peaches with vinaigrette. Yield: 6 servings.

Courtesy of Dickey Farms, Musella, Georgia, "The Sweetest Peaches in the South"

FRESH PEACH SQUASH CASSEROLE

2½ cups sliced yellow squash or zucchini
1 cup South Carolina peaches, sliced
2 tablespoons brown sugar
Salt and pepper to taste
2½ tablespoons butter

Preheat oven to 350 degrees. Spray a 2-quart casserole with nonstick cooking spray. Place layer of squash then layer of peaches in casserole. Continue alternating layers of fruit and vegetable until all have been used. Sprinkle brown sugar and salt over the dish and dot with butter. Cover and bake for 45 minutes to an hour. Serves 4.

Courtesy of South Carolina Peach Council

BAKED BEANS WITH A TWIST

An unexpected side dish to serve with barbecued beef

2 (16-ounce) cans baked beans
¼ cup dark corn syrup
¼ cup finely chopped onion
¼ teaspoon ground allspice
8 ripe Michigan peach halves
3 tablespoons orange marmalade

Preheat oven to 350 degrees. In a medium mixing bowl, using a plastic spatula, stir the beans, corn syrup, onion and allspice. Pour into a 1½-quart casserole and bake in preheated oven for 1 hour. Place peach halves, cut side up on top of beans. Gently spoon 1 tablespoon orange marmalade into each peach cavity. Place uncovered casserole back into oven for 15 minutes. Serves 8.

Tools of the orchard are treated as priceless jewels and handed down from one generation to the next. Models of orchard ladders (center). Photo Courtesy Dr. Paul Rood and the State Horticultural Society of Michigan.

PEACH BAVARIAN CREAM

2 tablespoons gelatin
½ cup cold water
1 quart sliced fresh peaches
1 cup sugar
¼ teaspoon salt
1 pint cream, whipped

Soak the gelatin in the cold water for 5 minutes. Mash the peaches with the sugar, rub through sieve, and simmer for five minutes. Remove from the stove, add softened gelatin and salt, and stir until the gelatin is dissolved. Chill, and when the mixture begins to thicken, fold in the whipped cream. Place in a wet mold, let stand in a cold place until firm, and turn out on a serving platter.

Optional: Garnish with red raspberry syrup drizzled on platter.

PEACH FLUFF SALAD

1 (8-ounce) can crushed pineapple
1 (4-serving) box peach-flavored gelatin
2 cups buttermilk
1 (8-ounce) tub frozen whipped topping

In a medium saucepan, heat pineapple until very hot, stirring constantly. Do not boil. Remove from heat; add dry gelatin. Add buttermilk and mix well. Chill until set. Remove from refrigerator. Fold in whipped topping. Chill before serving.

Courtesy of Sharon McFall, Busy Woman's Cookbook©

PEACH JELLO® DESSERT

1 (3-ounce) package peach Jello®
1 (16-ounce) can fruit cocktail
1 (8-ounce) package cream cheese

Dissolve Jello® in boiling water, per package directions. Drain fruit cocktail, reserving ¾ cup liquid. Add cold water to make ¾ cup if necessary. Add to Jello®. Soften cream cheese with beater, until creamy at room temperature. Add to Jello®. Add fruit cocktail and chill until firm. You can use graham cracker crumbs on bottom and top.

Thanks to Elaine Jensen, Spring Run Farm, Lowell, Indiana

LIBERTY HYDE BAILEY JR

On many summer mornings, a pearl-gray fog shrouds the valley areas of the Southwestern Michigan area known as the "Fruitbelt". The two lane back roads take you through flat areas of manicured grain crops, passing hundreds of areas of fruit trees and vineyards on hillsides – au characteristic of the glacial terrain. As the sun rises, the landscape awakens to a brilliant spectrum of glistening light. In these quiet outdoor spaces, millions of droplets work in tandem to magnify the intricacy of maturing peaches on the majestic trees.

Only the vast area known as Lake Michigan separates this paradise from Chicago. The "Great Lake" helps to temper the weather, the unique soil and other criteria have aided this agricultural treasure trove. William Burnett operated a trading post on the west bank of the St. Joseph River, one of only two rivers to flow northward in the U.S. He is credited with planting the first peach tree in

the area in the 1780's. The word spread of the great valley where fruit grew and by 1865 there were more than 207,000 peach trees and thousands of other fruit trees and grapevines masking the country side of Southwestern Michigan. Chicago's population had grown to just under 30,000 in 1850 and was only sixty-two miles away by boat from Benton Harbor, Michigan. This city had become the market place for fruit buyers and sellers. This was the start of the birthing process of the Benton Harbor Fruit Market in the early 1860's. In 1839 the first shipment of peaches left St. Joseph harbor by schooner to Chicago. A few short years later thousands of baskets of peaches were being shipped to Chicago annually.

By 1870 the railroad reached the Benton Harbor area and this opened new markets for the growers, that were really enjoying their "hey day". Then seven years later the first refrigerated railroad cars were introduced and this allowed the Georgia, South Carolina and New York growers to ship to Chicago. By this time most every type of fruit except for citrus was in production. So the growers had these other crops to carry them through when the fungus known as

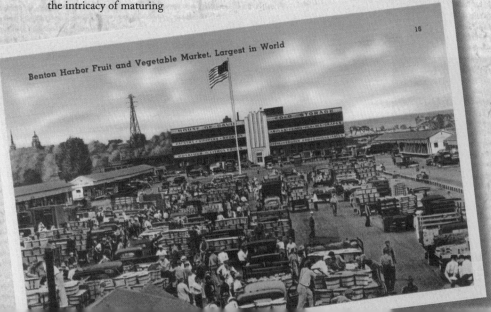

Benton Harbor Fruit and Vegetable Market. Largest in World

"the yellow" devastated the peach orchards of Southwestern Michigan. With new varieties being introduced Michigan Fruit Belt area made its come back. A prominent family in this area were the Liberty Hyde Baileys who migrated from Vermont in 1840. Their son Liberty Hyde Bailey Jr. graduated from Michigan Agricultural College in East Lansing, Michigan the first agricultural college in the country. He worked a few years with America's greatest botanist Asa Gray of Harvard. In 1888 he became professor of horticulture at Cornell University. By 1903 he became dean and director. He emphasized plant breeding and the improvement of new varieties, saying that "ultimately there must be varieties developed for every local region adapted to each region." He was the first president of the American Society for Horticultural Science, formed in 1903. Today it is the greatest horticultural research organization in the world. Past president of the American Pomological Society, the oldest fruit organization in America. He authored over one hundred books, and edited so many more. Cornell University payed honor to Dr. Bailey with the Construction of the L.H. Bailey Hortorium which houses the thousands of plant specimens he collected. The U.S. Government produced a postage stamp in his honor. In 1908 President Theodore Roosevelt appointed him chairman of the Commission on Country Life which under his leadership became the formation of the 4-H youth program and the Cooperative Extension Service. His birth place in South Haven, Michigan is now a museum.

South Haven is known for another horticulturist, Dr. Stanley Johnston. His father was a student of Dr. L.H. Bailey Jr. Dr. Johnston's plant research led him to develop the Haven varieties of which the Red Haven peach has become the world's best known peach. He was Director of the South Haven Experiment Station. He personally brought Michigan from raising no blueberries to being the nation's largest producer of blueberries. His many accomplishments and contributions to the horticultural industry all over the world were recognized when he was inducted into the American Society or Horticultural Science Hall of Fame. Many of the farms that dotted the landscape of the S.W. Michigan fruitbelt in the late 1800's are currently being farmed by fourth and fifth generation members of the original families. Some of these families and farms are pictured in this book. These pictures mirror a kaleidoscope of color, tree form, soil texture, light and shade. All of these leave an indelible mark on our souls and make us envy the artist that capture on canvas the fleeting vignettes of each of the peach farms.

A fancy load of peaches, (upper right) which Secretary Bassett found both pleasure and profit in marketing. Photo Courtesy Dr. Paul Rood and the State Horticultural Society of Michigan.

ANGEL SALAD WITH GEORGIA PEACH HALO (MOLD)

1 (29-ounce) can cling Georgia peach slices
¾ cup syrup reserved from peaches
1 envelope (1 tablespoon) plain gelatin
3 tablespoons lemon juice
2 (3-ounce) packages cream cheese
½ cup mayonnaise
¼ teaspoon salt
1 teaspoon prepared horseradish
½ cup chilled evaporated milk
½ cup finely chopped celery

Drain peaches; heat syrup to boiling. Soften gelatin in lemon juice and dissolve in hot syrup. Cool. Mash cheese with fork; blend in mayonnaise and seasonings. Blend in gelatin. Whip chilled evaporated milk in chilled bowl until fluffy. Fold in gelatin, celery and peach slices, withholding 7 slices for garnish. Turn into 8-inch ring mold and chill until firm. Unmold on greens. Decorate with peaches and berries or cherries. Serve with additional mayonnaise mixed with whipped cream, if desired. Yield: 8 to 10 servings.

Courtesy of Dickey Farms, Musella, Georgia, "The Sweetest Peaches in the South"

GEORGIA PEACH MELBA MOLD

1 (1-pound) can sliced Georgia peaches
2 tablespoons lemon juice
1 (3-ounce) package lemon flavored gelatin
2 teaspoons milk
2 tablespoons mayonnaise or salad dressing
1 (3 ounce) package cream cheese, softened
2 tablespoons finely chopped pecans
1 (10 ounce) package frozen red raspberries, thawed
2 tablespoons lemon juice
1 (3 ounce) package raspberry flavored gelatin

Peach layer: Drain peaches, reserving syrup. Combine syrup and 2 tablespoons lemon juice; add cold water to make 1 cup. Dissolve lemon gelatin in 1 cup hot water. Add syrup mixture; chill until partly set. Add peaches. Pour into 6½-cup ring mold. Chill until almost set.
Cheese layer: Mix milk, mayonnaise and cream cheese; stir in pecans. Spread cheese layer over peaches.
Raspberry layer: drain raspberries, reserving syrup. Combine syrup and lemon juice; add cold water to make 1 cup. Dissolve raspberry gelatin in 1 cup hot water; add syrup mixture. Chill until partially set. Stir in raspberries. Pour over cheese. Chill until firm. Turn mold over onto serving plate. Yield: 8 servings.

Courtesy of Dickey Farms, Musella, Georgia, "The Sweetest Peaches in the South"

STUFFED GEORGIA PEACH HALVES

- 4 medium Georgia peaches, peeled, halved and seeded
- 1 tablespoon lemon juice
- ½ teaspoon ground cinnamon
- 2 tablespoons vanilla low-fat yogurt
- 2 tablespoons unsweetened flaked coconut, toasted
- 2 teaspoons honey
- 2 tablespoons raisins
- 1 teaspoon vanilla extract
- ½ teaspoon grated lemon rind

Coat peach halves with lemon juice and set aside. Combine remaining ingredients; stir well. Spoon mixture into cavity of each peach half. Chill. Yield: 8 servings.

Courtesy of Dickey Farms, Musella, Georgia, "The Sweetest Peaches in the South"

TEXAS CHAMPAGNE PEACHES

- 2 cups dry champagne
- ½ cup sugar
- 1 tablespoon vanilla

Peaches, peeled, pitted and halved

Combine champagne and sugar in a saucepan. Bring to a boil. Add vanilla. Add peaches, cut side down. Cover. Reduce heat and simmer 4 minutes. Turn peaches and simmer again. After cooking, remove peaches and boil mixture to reduce. Pour over peach halves and chill.

Thanks to Martha Lewis, Canton, Texas

MARINATED FRESH FRUIT BOWL

½ cup honey
¼ cup water
¼ cup lime juice
¼ cup Triple Sec
1 cup watermelon balls
1 cup cantaloupe balls
2 large nectarines or Georgia peaches, peeled and sliced
½ cup strawberries, halved
1 cup honey dew melon balls
4 kiwi, peeled and sliced

In small saucepan, combine the honey and water. Bring to a boil. Reduce heat and simmer for 5 minutes. Stir in lime juice and Triple Sec. Cook completely. In a bowl, combine all fruit. Pour liquid mixture over fruit and mix gently. Cover and refrigerate for 2 hours to blend flavors.

Courtesy of Dickey Farms, Musella, Georgia, "The Sweetest Peaches in the South"

COLD FRUIT CASSEROLE

1 can pears
1 can peaches
1 can white cherries
1 can pineapple
1 can apricots
1 can spiced apples
1 stick margarine or butter
2 tablespoons flour
1 cup sherry wine

Drain juices from fruit. Pour fruit into a casserole dish. Melt butter, add flour and sherry. Mix well. Pour over fruit. Refrigerate 8 hours or overnight. Heat casserole in a 325 degree oven for about 30 minutes before serving.

Thanks to Bettye J. Knott, Waxahachie, Texas

Entrees

XIAN STIR FRY

½ cup almonds, slivered (or sliced)

2 tablespoons peanut oil

1½ pounds sirloin (or tenderloin), cut into strips

1 green pepper, seeded, cut into strips

1 yellow bell pepper, seeded, cut into strips

½ cup onion, chopped fine

1 teaspoon grated fresh ginger

6 fresh South Carolina peaches, peeled and cut into quarters

½ cup orange juice

2 tablespoons brown sugar

2 tablespoons hoisin sauce

⅛ teaspoon pepper

2 cups beef broth

½ cup white wine

5 tablespoon cornstarch

Place oil in the wok and add the slivered almonds. Toast until lightly golden. Add beef, peppers, onions and grated ginger. Stir fry for 1 minute. In a separate bowl, mix fresh peach slices with orange juice; set aside. Add brown sugar, hoisin sauce, pepper, and beef broth to wok and simmer for 1 minute. Mix corn starch with wine. Stir into the beef mixture and simmer. Add the peach and orange juice combination. Stir fry for 1 more minute. Serve on white rice or buckwheat noodles. Serves 8.

Courtesy of South Carolina Peach Council

FLANK STEAK WITH PEACHES

½ cup red wine

½ cup pureed South Carolina peaches

¼ cup reduced-sodium soy sauce

2 tablespoons sesame oil

1 South Carolina peach, pitted and sliced

3 cloves garlic, smashed

1 inch gingerroot, sliced, washed and peeled

1 (1½ pound) flank steak

2 tablespoons olive oil

Pulse red wine, puree, soy sauce, sesame oil, peach slices, garlic and ginger in a blender for 20 seconds. Pour into a 11 x 9-inch baking dish, add the steak, and turn to coat. Cover dish and marinate for 1–24 hours in the refrigerator, turning two or three times to marinate. Remove from refrigerator and allow to come to room temperature (about 30 minutes). Preheat grill to high. Pour off and reserve marinade from steak. Pour 2 tablespoons olive oil over steak and turn to coat. Place directly on the grill over heat. Baste the reserved marinade and grill 4 minutes on each side for medium rare, 5–7 minutes on each side for medium well. Let stand 5 minutes before cutting widthwise into thin slices with a sharp knife held at a 45-degree angle. Serves 4 to 6.

Courtesy of South Carolina Peach Council

(Opposite upper right) Orchard of Edwin H. House, Saugatuck, Michigan. Photo Courtesy Dr. Paul Rood and the State Horticultural Society of Michigan.

PEACHY PORK TENDERLOIN

1 (12-ounce) pork tenderloin
⅓ cup peach nectar
3 tablespoons light teriyaki sauce
2 tablespoons snipped fresh rosemary, crushed
1 tablespoon olive oil

Place pork in a plastic bag and set in a shallow dish. Marinade is prepared in a small bowl by combining peach nectar, teriyaki sauce, rosemary and olive oil. Pour over pork. Close bag, place in refrigerator for 4 to 24 hours, turning bag occasionally. Drain pork and discard marinade. Serves 4.

   Place on grill for about 30 minutes or until no pink remains and juices run clear.

Thanks to Bettye J. Knott, Waxahachie, Texas

PORK CUTLETS WITH BOURBON GLAZED PEACHES AND ONIONS OVER CREAMY GRITS

FOR THE PORK

- 1 cup flour
- Salt and pepper
- Oil
- 5 (6-ounce) pork cutlets cut from a tenderloin
- 6 South Carolina peaches, cut into eighths and peeled
- ½ red onion, sliced
- 2 tablespoons sugar
- 2 ounces butter
- 6 ounces Bourbon (such as Maker's Mark)

FOR THE GRITS

- 3 cups water
- 1 cup heavy cream
- 1 cup grits
- Salt and pepper
- 8 ounces cream cheese

Pork Cutlets: Heat a sauté pan. Add some oil. Season flour with salt and pepper. Dredge the pork cutlets and sauté in the oil. Set aside when done. Wipe out the pan, add fresh oil. Drop in the onions and season. As they start to cook, sprinkle with 1 tablespoon sugar. When the sugar melts and the onions begin to brown add the peaches. Add another tablespoon sugar and let caramelize. Add the bourbon and flame off. Season and finish by swirling in cold butter.

Grits: Bring the water and cream to a boil. Stir in the grits and season. Turn the grits down to a simmer. Simmer until cooked. Stir in Cream Cheese and check seasoning.

To serve: place a bed of grits on the plate. Lean the pork on the grits. Top the pork with the peaches and onions. Serves 4.

Recipe courtesy of Chef Robert Stegall-Smith. Corporate Chef for Institution Food House. Published by South Carolina Peach Council

GRILLED PEACHES AND PORK

4 boneless lean pork chops, trimmed

2 tablespoons balsamic vinegar

2 tablespoons lime juice

½ teaspoon chili power

3 teaspoons fresh thyme

1 tablespoon brown sugar

½ teaspoon salt

½ teaspoon pepper

4 large South Carolina peaches

2 tablespoons balsamic vinegar

6 cups fresh baby spinach

1 teaspoon sugar

Using a rolling pan, carefully pound pork chops until they are ¼-inch thick. Combine 2 tablespoons vinegar, lime juice, chili power, thyme, sugar, salt, and pepper. Set aside 2 tablespoons of the marinade. Pour remaining marinade into a sealable plastic bag. Add pork and marinate for 2 hours. Turn once. Preheat grill at medium. Bring a large pot of water to boil. Dunk peaches in boiling water for 10 seconds each. Peel off loosened skin and halve peaches. Remove pit. Drizzle peach halves with 2 tablespoons balsamic vinegar. Remove pork from plastic bag. Place on grill. Grill for 3 minutes on each side basting with the bagged marinade. Place cooked pork on clean plate and keep warm. Throw out bagged marinade. Grab a sheet of tin foil. Spray with cooking spray. Place on grill. Cook peaches, pit side down, for 4 minutes. Flip over and cook 2 more minutes, until hot. Remove from grill. Slice each half into 4 slices. Place clean baby spinach in a large bowl. Drizzle with the remaining 2 tablespoons marinade. Toss. Place equal amounts of spinach on 4 plates. Top with a pork chops and peaches. Sprinkle with sugar. Serves 4.

Courtesy of South Carolina Peach Council

CENTER CUT PORK CHOPS WITH CALIFORNIA CLING PEACH TERIYAKI GLAZE

Peach glaze can also be served with chicken breasts

4 center cut pork chops (8– 10-ounces each)

PEACH TERIYAKI GLAZE

¼ cup Tamari soy sauce

6 tablespoons light brown sugar

3 tablespoons rice wine vinegar

¼ teaspoon ground ginger

2 teaspoons fresh garlic, minced

2 tablespoons onion, finely minced

1 tablespoon cornstarch, dissolved in one tablespoon water

1 (15-ounce) can California cling peaches in light syrup, drained

1 tablespoon sliced almonds

1 tablespoon fresh basil leaves, chopped

Salt and freshly ground pepper to taste

MARINADE

2 tablespoons Tamari soy sauce

1½ teaspoons dry mustard (optional)

2 tablespoons canola oil for sautéing

Peach Teriyaki Glaze Preparation: Heat the soy sauce, brown sugar, rice wine vinegar and ginger in a 4-quart saucepan over medium heat. Add the garlic and onion and simmer gently for 3 or 4 minutes. Stir in the cornstarch, lower the heat and whisk until the teriyaki glaze has thickened, about 20 seconds. Carefully stir in the California Cling Peaches with a rubber spatula, taking care to bathe them completely in the glaze. Gently simmer for another minute to warm the peaches. Note: This glaze can be made in advance and reheated for service.

Pork Chops Preparation: For the marinade, whisk the soy sauce into the dry mustard in a stainless steel bowl. Toss the pork chops in this mixture and drain well. Heat the canola oil in a large skillet over medium heat and sauté the pork chops for 8 to 10 minutes on each side. (The pork chops may also be grilled or baked.) Remove from skillet, season generously with salt and ground pepper and allow to rest for 3 minutes. Place the pork chops onto 4 warmed plates and top with Peach Teriyaki Glaze. Garnish with sliced almonds and basil. Serve immediately. Makes: 4 servings.

Courtesy of the California Cling Peach Board and Gary Jenanyan

GRILLED PORK CHOPS WITH GEORGIA PEACH TOMATO BBQ SAUCE

To keep the pork chops from burning, rotate them from the hottest parts of the grill to the perimeter during cooking, basting with barbecue sauce as you do so.

1 tablespoon olive oil

1 medium onion, finely chopped

1 clove garlic, minced

1 (1-inch) piece ginger, peeled and grated

1½ cups canned tomato sauce

½ cup best-quality peach jam

2 Georgia peaches, peeled and cut into ¾-inch chunks

1 to 2 tablespoons sherry vinegar

Salt and freshly ground black pepper

4 pork chops (6 to 8 ounces each) trimmed of fat

Heat olive oil in a medium saucepan over medium heat. Add chopped onion and cook until translucent, about 2 minutes. Add minced garlic and ginger; cook about 2 minutes more. Stir in tomato sauce, peach jam, and peaches. Reduce heat to low; simmer until sauce thickens, about 30 minutes. Stir in vinegar to taste. Adjust seasoning with salt and pepper. Remove from heat; let cool. Pour half the barbecue sauce into a shallow baking dish, add pork chops, turning to coat both sides. Reserve remaining sauce. Grill pork chops on a medium-hot grill or grill pan until chops are well marked and cooked through, at least 5 minutes per side. Baste chops with barbecue sauce; rotate during cooking. Remove from grill. Let stand about 10 minutes before serving. Serve with remaining sauce. Yield: 4 servings.

Courtesy of Dickey Farms, Musella, Georgia, "The Sweetest Peaches in the South"

BBQ PORK CHOPS AND PEACHES

3 cups chopped peeled peaches
1 cup dry white wine
¼ cup sugar
1 teaspoon salt, divided
¼ teaspoon pepper, divided
2 tablespoons white vinegar
2 tablespoons molasses
1 teaspoon chili pepper
½ teaspoon paprika
¼ teaspoon ground red pepper
6 (6-ounce) bone-in center cut pork chops, trimmed
6 South Carolina peaches, halved, pitted

Combine first 3 ingredients in a small saucepan; bring to boil. Cover, reduce heat, and simmer 25 minutes. Uncover and simmer 5 minutes. Place mixture into food processor; process until smooth. Add ¾ teaspoon salt, dash of black pepper, vinegar, and next 4 ingredients; pulse to combine. Let stand 5 minutes. Place half of mixture in a large Ziploc freezer bag; reserve other half for basting. Add chops to bag; seal, and refrigerate 30 minutes to 4 hours. Remove pork from bag; discard marinade. Sprinkle pork with remaining salt and another dash of black pepper. Place pork and peach halves on grill rack coated with cooking spray. Grill pork on an open grill over medium high heat for 10 minutes or until pork is done and peaches are tender, turning once. Baste pork and peach halves with reserved peach sauce every 2 minutes during first 6 minutes of cooking. Serves 6.

Courtesy of South Carolina Peach Council

BBQ SPARE RIBS WITH PEACHES

- 3 pounds country spareribs
- 1 teaspoon salt
- 3 cups South Carolina peaches, peeled and sliced
- ¼ cup brown sugar
- 1 cup ketchup
- 2 tablespoons Worcestershire sauce
- 1 tablespoon dried onion or ¼ cup chopped onion
- 2 tablespoons flour
- 2 tablespoons yellow mustard
- ½ teaspoon ground cloves
- 1 teaspoon salt
- ½ teaspoon black pepper

Preheat oven to 375 degrees. In shallow roast pan, place ribs and sprinkle with 1 teaspoon salt. Mash or blend 1 cup of the peaches into a puree. Place the remaining 2 cups peaches into a separate bowl and sprinkle with brown sugar. In saucepan, combine mashed peaches, ketchup, Worcestershire sauce, onion, flour, mustard, cloves, salt, and pepper. Heat to boiling and pour over ribs. Bake about 1½ to 2 hours, turning ribs once. Add peaches and juice 35 minutes before removing from oven.

Courtesy of South Carolina Peach Council

BROILED CANNED PEACHES

Drain halves of large canned peaches from the syrup, place in a shallow baking dish, pit side up, pour over them a small quantity of melted butter, and add a very little salt. Broil in oven until the peaches are tender and lightly browned. Serve hot with the meat course.

PEACH LAMB CHOPS

12 lamb loin chops (1-inch thick)
¼ teaspoon salt
¼ teaspoon garlic powder
2 tablespoons Dijon-mayonnaise blend
2 tablespoons brown sugar
½ cup peach nectar
2 tablespoons minced fresh mint
⅔ cup dried peaches, sliced or minced

Sprinkle lamb chops with salt and garlic powder. Rub each side of chops with Dijon-mayonnaise blend and sprinkle with brown sugar. In a large nonstick skillet coated with cooking spray, brown chops on both sides over medium-high heat. Add apricot nectar and mint. Reduce heat; cover and simmer for 12–15 minutes. Add peaches. Simmer, uncovered, 5 minutes longer or until meat reaches desired doneness and sauce is slightly thickened. Serve sauce over lamb. Yield: 6 servings.

Courtesy of South Carolina Peach Council

FRUITED CHICKEN

1 large onion, sliced
6 boneless skinless chicken breast halves
⅓ cup orange juice
2 tablespoons soy sauce
2 tablespoons Worcestershire sauce
2 tablespoons Dijon mustard
1 tablespoon grated orange peel
2 garlic cloves, minced
½ cup chopped dried peaches
½ cup dried cranberries
Hot cooked rice

Place onion and chicken in a 5-quart slow cooker. Combine the orange juice, soy sauce, Worcestershire sauce, mustard, orange peel and garlic; pour over chicken. Sprinkle with peaches and cranberries. Cover and cook on low for 7–8 hours or until chicken juices run clear. Serve over rice. Yield: 6 servings.

Courtesy of South Carolina Peach Council

GINGER AND GEORGIA PEACH CHICKEN

4 small skinless, boneless chicken breast
halves

1 (8-ounce) can peach slices in light syrup

1 teaspoon cornstarch

¼ teaspoon salt

½ (8-ounce) can sliced water chestnuts,
drained

2 cups hot cooked rice

½ teaspoon grated fresh ginger*

1 (6-ounce) package frozen pea pods,
cooked and drained

*⅛ teaspoon ground ginger may be substituted.

Coat a large skillet with nonstick vegetable spray. Preheat skillet over medium heat. Add chicken. Cook over medium heat for 8 to 10 minutes or until tender and no longer pink, turning to brown evenly. Remove chicken from skillet; keep warm. Meanwhile drain peaches, reserving juice. Add water to juice to equal ½ cup. Stir in cornstarch, ginger, and salt. Add to skillet. Cook and stir until thickened and bubbly. Cook and stir 1 minute more. Gently stir in peaches and water chestnuts; heat through. On a serving platter or 4 individual plates, arrange rice, pea pods, and chicken. Spoon sauce over chicken.

Courtesy of Dickey Farms, Musella, Georgia, "The Sweetest Peaches in the South"

VOGEL ORCHARD

Vogel Orchard is one of the oldest orchards in the "Hill Country" of Texas. Starting in 1900 with just a few trees, the farm had grown to 300 trees by 1953. Many of these peaches were shipped to San Antonio. Later customers wanted to drive to see the orchards so the Vogels introduced the first roadside stand and that turned into a u-pick business. It became an outing for the city families.

In 1997 Jamey Vogel, a CPA by profession, and his wife moved back to the area to care for the farm due to his father's poor health. Jamie is now devoting full time to 3,000 peach trees, 900 blackberries and plums. The beauty of their farm, the quality of their fruit and the national attention Fredericksburg, Texas has received brought Southern Living Magazine to do a feature article on Vogels Orchard.

GRILLED CHICKEN WITH SPIKED PEACH GLAZE

Olive oil

Salt and freshly ground pepper

  8 skinless chicken breasts

Peach Glaze

  4 ripe South Carolina peaches, cut in half and pitted

PEACH GLAZE:

  2 cups peach preserves or jam

  1 tablespoon finely chopped garlic

  3 tablespoons olive oil

  2 tablespoons soy sauce

  1 tablespoon Dijon mustard

  1 small jalapeno, finely chopped

Combine Peach Glaze ingredients in a medium bowl and season with salt and pepper to taste. Reserve ½ cup. Preheat grill. Brush the chicken with olive oil and season with salt and pepper to taste. Place on grill and cook for 6 to 7 minutes, until golden brown. Turn over and continue cooking for 5 to 6 minutes. Brush both sides with the peach glaze and continue cooking an additional 4 to 5 minutes. Place tin foil sprayed with nonstick cooking spray on grill. Place peach halves on tin foil, cut side down and grill for 2 minutes. Turn over and brush with the reserved ½ cup of peach glaze, grill for 3 to 4 more minutes until peaches are soft.

Courtesy of South Carolina Peach Council

JULIE'S PISTACHIO AND PEACH CHICKEN

5 *South Carolina peaches, peeled and sliced*

2 *tablespoons sugar*

1 *tablespoon lemon juice*

4 *whole chicken breasts*

1 *cup pistachio nuts, ground fine (you may need more)*

3 *tablespoons plain fine ground bread crumbs*

4 *tablespoons sherry*

4 *tablespoons butter*

4 *tablespoons sunflower oil*

Mix peach slices, sugar and lemon juice. Set aside. Skin, bone, halve and butterfly each breast. You will have 16 pieces total. Wash and pat chicken dry. Mix nuts and bread crumbs together. Dip each chicken half into ground nuts and bread crumbs mixture. Let sit several minutes to dry. Melt butter and oil in medium heavy skillet. Brown each chicken breast quickly. Remove each breast when done. Pour small amount of juice from peaches into skillet and heat 1 minute. Add sherry. Place breasts back into skillet. Cover and simmer about 15 minutes, turning once. After 10 minutes, add peaches and their juice; cover. Let cook remaining 5 minutes. Before serving, sprinkle with extra pistachio nuts, if desired. Serve each person 2 halves and several peach pieces each.

Courtesy of South Carolina Peach Council

GEORGIA PEACH PARMESAN CHICKEN

    4 halves boneless, skinless chicken breasts
    2 tablespoons Dijon mustard
   ¼ pound prosciutto, thinly sliced
    2 tablespoons flour
   ½ teaspoon tarragon
   ½ cup finely ground bread crumbs
   ⅓ cup grated parmesan cheese
    1 egg, lightly beaten
    4 tablespoons butter, divided
    3 fresh Georgia peaches, sliced
    4 tablespoons white wine

Place chicken breasts between layers of waxed paper and pound to ⅛-inch thickness. Spread mustard on one side of chicken and top with prosciutto. Roll up chicken breasts and secure with toothpicks. In separate shallow dishes, mix flour with tarragon, bread crumbs and parmesan cheese. Dip chicken roll-ups in flour mixture, then in egg, then in bread crumb mixture. Melt 2 tablespoons of butter in an 8 x 8-inch baking pan. Place roll-ups in pan and bake at 375 degrees for 20 minutes. Add peach slices. Melt remaining butter and mix with wine; sprinkle over chicken. Bake 15 minutes more. Serve with pan juices. Yield: 4 servings

Courtesy of Dickey Farms, Musella, Georgia, "The Sweetest Peaches in the South"

OVEN FRIED CHICKEN AND PEACHES

   ½ cup crushed bran flakes
   ¼ cup sunflower seeds, chopped
   ½ teaspoon seasoned salt
4–6 chicken breast halves
    4 South Carolina peaches, peeled and sliced into quarters
   ¼ cup butter, melted
    2 tablespoons lemon juice

Combine bran flakes, seeds and seasoned salt. In another dish, combine the melted butter and lemon juice. Dip chicken pieces in butter mixture, then in bran mixture to coat the pieces evenly. Reserve remaining butter and bran flake mixture. Place chicken into baking pan and bake at 350 degrees for 1 hour. Mix together remaining butter and bran flakes mixture. Stir in peaches. After the chicken has been in the oven for 30 minutes, add the peach mixture. Continue to cook for the remaining 30 minutes.

Courtesy of South Carolina Peach Council

SUMMER CHICKEN SALAD

  1 (12-ounce) package frozen rice pilaf
¼ cup light mayonnaise
¼ cup sour cream or yogurt
¼ cup chopped green bell pepper
  2 tablespoons sliced green onion
½ teaspoon dried tarragon
¼ teaspoon dried dill weed
Salt and black pepper to taste
  2 cups chopped cooked chicken (canned or fresh)
  4 fresh South Carolina peaches, peeled and sliced
Large lettuce leaves that look like cups

Prepare rice pilaf according to package directions; cool in mixing bowl. Stir in mayonnaise through black pepper. Add chicken; toss lightly to coat. Cover and chill until ready to use. Shortly before serving, add peaches and toss. Serve in lettuce cups. Serves 4.

Courtesy of South Carolina Peach Council

CHICKEN AND PEACH SALAD

1½ pounds boneless, skinless chicken breast halves, cut into strips
  2 tablespoons Cajun seasoning
  2 tablespoons olive oil
  6 cups salad greens
6 or 7 medium peaches, peeled and sliced (about 3 cups)
  1 medium red onion, thinly sliced
  1 cup raspberry vinaigrette (such as Newman's Lighten Up Raspberry and Vinaigrette and Walnut Dressing)

Put chicken and Cajun seasoning in a zip lock plastic bag and shake. Warm oil in skillet over medium heat. Add chicken and cook 10–12 minutes, stirring often. Remove chicken from skillet and set aside. Toss greens, peaches, onion, and vinaigrette in a large salad bowl. Add chicken and serve. Serves 6.

Thanks to Bettye J. Knott, Waxahachie, Texas

J. Barber, 1871

Capt. Selah Dustin had plenty of luck and too much of it was bad. Born in Claremont, New Hampshire in 1817, Dustin left home at age nineteen and moved to Detroit where he became a sailor. By the early 1850's he had his own ship. His business was successful until competition forced him to retreat from the fight bruised and bloodied, with most of his fortune gone. With the last of his hopes and money, he bought the steamer J. Barber.

Built in Cleveland, Ohio in 1856 for the lumber trade, the Barber had spent several years plying a route from Milwaukee to Manistee, Michigan. Businessman Nathan Engleman of Milwaukee bought her in 1865 and had her rebuilt at the shipyard of Allen and McClelland, for the considerable sum of $14,000 ($285,700 in 2006 dollars). Afterward, she carried lumber and passengers between Milwaukee and Manistee, Michigan with such success that

within three years Engleman had a fleet of six steamers running back and forth across Lake Michigan. Engleman sold the Barber to Dustin in 1871 and he in turn chartered her to James Paxton and Curtis Broughton of St. Joseph, Michigan. By that time, the Barber had seen better days. Despite the extensive renovations of a few years before, she carried only a B-1 rating and many sailors considered her unseaworthy. Major mishaps did not stop the Barber. On the evening of July 18, 1871 her decks were crammed with peaches from Berrien County Michigan orchards destined for market in Chicago. The J. Barber's two passengers and many of her crew turned in for the night soon after leaving St. Joseph, Michigan. Capt. James E. Snow retired to his cabin to read, leaving the command of the ship to the first mate, George Germain.

At about 12:30AM, flames suddenly burst out on the deck near the smokestack. Ship's porter J.C. Nesbitt and Steward Harrie Watcher were asleep in their cabins near the smokestack when First Mate Germain pounded down the hallway, yelling "fire!"

Grand Rapids Market before 6 AM. Photo Courtesy Dr. Paul Rood and the State Horticultural Society of Michigan.

Both men toppled out of their bunks and tried to pull on their clothing, but the fire spread so quickly they had to abandon their cabin before they could fully dress. Captain Snow ran onto the deck at the first alarm. He ordered the J. Barber's engines stopped, but the flames raced so rapidly through the vessel that no time remained to organize fire fighting efforts. Instead, Snow gave the order to abandon ship and called on the crew to lower lifeboats. Nesbitt and Watcher went to help, but the lifeboats hung on davits near the smokestack, and the men were forced to give up when the flames erupted through the deck, setting the lifeboats on fire.

Now desperate, Captain Snow called on his crew to toss anything overboard that would float, including furniture, boards and doors. He planned to use the debris as life rafts. The ship's cook caused amusement in the midst of terror. He wielded an ax to cut away some doors and threw them overboard. When he leapt into the lake after them, he landed directly on a door and fell through to his waist. The sight of the uninjured cook paddling about in the water, stuck halfway through the door and wearing a life preserver, tickled the watchman's funny bone.

The cook was the only object of amusement that evening. Two crewmen, watchman Pat Washington and deck hand Charles Brown, never made it to safety and their bodies were never recovered. The fire burned J. Barber nearly to the water line. About an hour after the blaze broke out, the hull slipped beneath the surface of Lake Michigan and settled to its grave in 80 feet of water, some 10 miles from Michigan City, Indiana.

When Selah Dustin learned about the loss of the J. Barber, something inside the old New Hampshireman's mind snapped. The steamer had been worth $12,000 ($244,800 in 2006 dollars) and her cargo $7,500 ($153,000 in 2006 dollard); she was insured for exactly two-thirds of that amount. Dustin, therefore, had lost the enormous sum of $6,500 ($133,000 in 2006 dollars!) He became, in the quaint term of the day, "an eccentric". He abandoned his family and his business interests and took up the humble occupation of an express wagon driver. For many years, the odd, weather-beaten, ragged man was a familiar sight on the streets of Detroit. His only friend seemed to be the sinewy little mare that pulled the wagon. He brooded over the fortune he had lost in the shipping business, and now and then erupted into "violent outburst when fits of rage overcame him". His peculiarities finally resulted in an attempt to have the courts declare him mentally incompetent. The judge deemed the old man legally sane, but Selah Dustin's final victory was short lived. He suffered a stroke that summer and died at St. Mary's hospital in Detroit on August 13, 1888 at the age of 71.

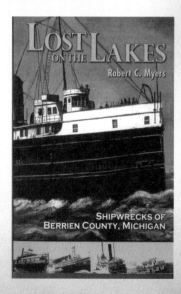

A DAY IN THE APPLE ORCHARD, COLOMA, MICH. 6004

GEORGIA PEACHY CHICKEN SALAD

⅓ cup mayonnaise
2 tablespoons milk
½ teaspoon salt
¼ teaspoon pepper
1 teaspoon chopped fresh tarragon*
2½ cups cubed cooked chicken
1 cup seedless red grapes, halved
1 cup frozen tiny peas, thawed
2 large Georgia peaches, peeled and chopped
1 cup pecan halves, toasted
Lettuce leaves

In a large bowl, stir the mayonnaise, milk, salt, pepper and tarragon until smooth. Add chicken and toss to coat. Stir in the grapes, peas, peaches and pecans. Serve in a lettuce-lined bowl. Yield: 4-6 servings.

* ¼ teaspoon dried tarragon may be substituted for fresh tarragon.

Courtesy of Dickey Farms, Musella, Georgia, "The Sweetest Peaches in the South"

PEACH SUPPER SALAD

2 large fresh South Carolina peaches, peeled and halved

2 teaspoons lemon juice

Romaine lettuce

1 cup diced cooked chicken

2 green onions, sliced

Curry dressing, see recipe

2 medium tomatoes, peeled and chopped

2 hard cooked eggs, chopped

2 slices crisply cooked bacon, crumbled

½ avocado, diced

CURRY DRESSING:

½ cup sour cream or mayonnaise

2 tablespoons milk

¼ teaspoon curry powder

Dash salt

1 teaspoon wine vinegar

Salad: Sprinkle peach halves with lemon juice; set aside. Line large individual salad bowls with Romaine leaves. Mix chicken and onion with enough curry dressing to moisten. Arrange peach halves in center of lettuce. Top each with a mound of chicken salad. Arrange remaining ingredients around peaches. Serve cold with extra curry dressing. Serves 2.

Curry Dressing: Blend sour cream and milk. Stir in remaining ingredients. Makes about ⅓ cup dressing.

Courtesy of South Carolina Peach Council

At Eden Springs House of David

DUCK AND PEACH SALAD ENTRÉE

8 tablespoons extra virgin olive oil
8 slices prosciutto
¼ teaspoon salt
¼ teaspoon freshly ground black pepper
8 duck breasts
4 medium ripe peaches
1 medium red onion
32 cherry tomatoes, halved
¾ cup pine nuts
1 bunch basil leaves
1 bunch wild rocket greens
2 tablespoons balsamic vinegar
1 long loaf crusty French bread

Preheat oven to 400 degrees. Heat 2 tablespoons extra virgin olive oil in frying pan in preparation to fry prosciutto until crisp; fully drain on paper towels. Simultaneously, salt and pepper duck breasts, then brown them in a large frying pan for 10–15 minutes in the oven. Wash and pat dry peaches; cut them into quarters; remove pit and slice peaches and red onion. Place peaches and onion slices on each plate, piled on one side; layer tomatoes and pine nuts over peaches and onions. Arrange basil and wild rocket greens next to peach mixture. Divide slices of hot duck breast on each plate alongside salad. Stir together reserve of olive oil and balsamic vinegar, dash of salt and pepper, sprinkle over entire dish. Sprinkle crumbled prosciutto over top.

Serve with warm French bread. Makes a beautiful presentation with greens, reds, golds and tender pink duck breast.

Four acres, Elberta Peach Trees bore a crop selling for $6,400 – 1899. (2006 value is $148,837.00). Photo Courtesy Dr. Paul Rood and the State Horticultural Society of Michigan.

CRAB CAKES WITH PEACH THYME CHUTNEY

CRAB CAKES

- 1 pound jumbo lump crabmeat
- 1½ cups bread crumbs, divided
- ¾ cup light mayonnaise
- 2 tablespoons fresh lemon juice
- 1 tablespoon chopped cilantro
- 1 tablespoon thinly sliced green onion

Salt and black pepper

- ½ cup canola oil

Peach Thyme Chutney (recipe follows)

PEACH THYME CHUTNEY

- 1 tablespoon butter
- 3 South Carolina peaches, peeled, pitted, and diced to ¼-inch
- ¼ cup firmly packed brown sugar
- ¼ cup white wine
- 1 tablespoon finely chopped fresh thyme leaves

Crab cakes: Mix crab, ¾ cup bread crumbs, mayonnaise, juice, cilantro, and scallions in a large mixing bowl. Season with salt and pepper to taste. Form the mixture into 8 cakes and coat with remaining bread crumbs. Refrigerate 20–30 minutes while making the chutney. Preheat the oven to 400 degrees. Pour oil into a large deep skillet and heat over medium-high heat. Place crab cakes into the hot oil and cook for 2 minutes. Flip and cook 5 minutes longer, or until golden brown. Remove from oil with a slotted spatula and place on a baking tray. Bake 5 minutes to finish. Place 2 cakes on each plate and serve with chutney. Serves 4.

Chutney: Brown butter slightly in a medium sauté pan over medium heat. Mix in peaches. Add sugar and stir 2 minutes, until dissolved. When sugar has formed a glaze over the peaches, add wine and cook 4–5 minutes, or until a syrup forms. Sprinkle in chopped thyme. Cook and stir, 1 minute longer. Remove from heat. Puree ½ cup chutney in a blender. Pour puree back into pan with remaining chutney and let cool. Serve with crab cakes or refrigerate up to 1 week. Makes 2 cups.

Courtesy of South Carolina Peach Council

SHRIMP AND GEORGIA PEACH STIR-FRY

2 tablespoons vegetable oil
1 pound large shrimp, shelled, deveined
½ pound broccoli, stems diagonally sliced
1 (8-ounce) can water chestnuts, drained, sliced
2 fresh Georgia peaches, sliced
3 green onions, diagonally sliced flowerets cut into bite-size pieces
Glossy Sauce (recipe follows)

Heat 1 tablespoon oil in wok or large skillet. Add shrimp and stir-fry until tender, about 4 to 5 minutes. Remove from wok; set aside. Add 1 tablespoon oil and stir-fry broccoli until tender-crisp, about 4 to 5 minutes. Add shrimp, water chestnuts, peaches and onions to wok and heat through. Stir in sauce and cook just until thick and glossy. Yield: 4 servings.

GLOSSY SAUCE

1½ tablespoons cornstarch
¾ cup chicken broth
⅓ cup sherry
1 teaspoon soy sauce
½ teaspoon minced fresh ginger root
1 teaspoon sugar.

Blend all ingredients.

Courtesy of Dickey Farms, Musella, Georgia, "The Sweetest Peaches in the South"

SHRIMP, PROSCIUTTO AND CALIFORNIA CLING PEACH SANDWICH

CHEESE SAUCE INGREDIENTS

- 2 tablespoons butter
- 2 tablespoons flour
- 1 cup milk
- ¾ cup grated Cheddar cheese
- ½ teaspoon Dijon mustard

SANDWICH INGREDIENTS

- 1 loaf, round sourdough bread
- 8 slices prosciutto
- ½ pound fresh shrimp, cooked
- 1 (15-ounce) can California cling peach slices

Cheese Sauce Preparation: In a small saucepan, heat butter over moderately low heat until melted. When butter is melted, stir in flour. Cook the paste, stirring constantly for about 2 minutes. Add milk, stirring for about 2 minutes or until sauce thickens. Add cheese and mustard and stir until cheese is melted. Keep sauce warm, covered over very low heat.

Sandwich Preparation: Cut four slices of sourdough bread, ¾-inch thick, and toast on baking sheet in oven. Lightly fry prosciutto until crispy, about 1 minute. Divide prosciutto among bread slices, top with shrimp and cheese sauce. Arrange peach slices on top. Makes 4 sandwiches

Courtesy of the California Cling Peach Board

CURRIED HALIBUT
WITH TOASTED PEACHES

1 pound halibut steaks
½ teaspoon curry powder
½ teaspoon grated onion
3 tablespoons butter
2 South Carolina peaches, halved
⅓ cup bread crumbs
⅓ cup grated cheese
2 tablespoons butter, melted

Mix curry powder, grated onion, and butter. Spread part of the mixture on halibut steaks and broil about 10 minutes. Season with salt; turn and spread with rest of curry butter and finish broiling. Sprinkle peach halves with dry sifted bread crumbs and grated cheese mixed (use equal portions). Drizzle peach halves with melted butter. Broil along with fish after fish has been turned.

Courtesy of South Carolina Peach Council

PEACH QUICHE

A very rich entree.

1 cup water, divided
6 medium ripe peaches
1½ teaspoons vanilla extract, divided
¾ cup chopped almonds, optional
1 (9–10-inch) pie crust, baked and cooled
3 eggs
1 cup whipping cream
2 tablespoons bourbon

Preheat oven to 350 degrees. Bring ½ cup water to a boil. Use a slotted spoon and place peaches in boiling water. Blanch for about 1 minute. Peel, cut in half, remove stone and then cut into quarters. Set aside. Bring ½ cup water and 1 teaspoon vanilla extract to a boil. Poach peaches in syrup until peaches are cooked, but still firm. If using almonds, sprinkle them over the bottom of the cooked pie crust. Drain peaches and arrange in crust. Lightly beat eggs. Stir in cream, bourbon, remaining sugar and vanilla. Bake in a preheated 350 degree oven until custard is set. Cool on rack. Serves 6–8.

Thanks to Bettye J. Knott, Waxahachie, Texas

Breakfast & Breads

PEACH OMELET

- 1 cup peeled, sliced peaches
- 2 tablespoons lemon juice
- 4 slices bacon
- 2 tablespoons water
- 6 eggs or 1½ cups egg substitute
- 1 teaspoon chopped fresh chives
- ¼ teaspoon salt
- 1 tablespoon white sugar
- ⅛ teaspoon ground black pepper
- 1 pinch paprika

Mix peaches with lemon juice; set aside. Place bacon in a large, deep skillet. Cook over medium high heat until evenly brown. Drain, crumble and set aside. Reserve 1 tablespoon bacon grease in skillet. In a large bowl, mix together crumbled bacon, water, eggs, chives, salt, sugar and black pepper. Reheat bacon grease over medium high heat. When grease is hot, pour egg batter into pan. Arrange peach slices on top of egg batter. Cover and cook over medium heat for 1 minute. Uncover and cook until set. Sprinkle with paprika. Let cool slightly before serving. Serves 3.

Courtesy of South Carolina Peach Council

GEORGIA PEACH FRENCH TOAST COBBLER

1 (1-pound) loaf French bread, do not slice
5 eggs
½ cup milk
¼ teaspoon baking powder
1 teaspoon vanilla
½ cup sugar
1 teaspoon cinnamon
1 teaspoon cornstarch
4½ cups sliced fresh peaches
2 tablespoons butter, melted
Confectioners' sugar

Slice bread into eight (¾– 1-inch thick) slices; arrange in a shallow baking pan. In a bowl, whisk eggs, milk, baking powder and vanilla together and pour over bread, turning to coat evenly. Cover pan with plastic wrap; let stand for 2 hours at room temperature or overnight in the refrigerator. Preheat oven to 450 degrees. Spray a 13 x 9-inch baking pan with cooking spray. In a bowl, mix sugar, cinnamon and cornstarch. Gently stir in peaches until well-coated. Spread three-fourths of the peach mixture in prepared pan; place bread slices on top of peaches. Brush tops of bread with butter. Bake for 20–25 minutes or until toast is golden and peaches are bubbling. To serve, place toast slices on plates; top with a portion of the remaining peach mixture and sprinkle with confectioners' sugar.

Courtesy of Dickey Farms, Musella, Georgia, "The Sweetest Peaches in the South"

Winter nights were spent planning and buying from catalogs for spring planting.

Old barn door (opposite) that hung on the author's father's farm.

OLD TIMEY PEACH BREAD

2 cups flour
½ cup sugar
½ cup firmly packed brown sugar
⅛ teaspoon salt
1 teaspoon baking soda
2 cups South Carolina mashed peaches, approximately 1½ pounds very ripe fresh peaches
1 large egg, slightly beaten
2 tablespoons butter, melted
½ cup raisins or almonds
Glaze

In a bowl, mix together flour, sugars, salt and baking soda. Drain mashed peaches and put in large bowl. Add beaten egg and melted butter. Stir in raisins or nuts. Stir in flour mixture. Pour into greased and floured 9 x 5-inch loaf pan. Let stand 20 minutes. Bake at 350 degrees for 45 to 55 minutes. Cool in pan 15 minutes and finish cooling on wire rack. Drizzle with glaze.

GLAZE

1 cup confectioners' sugar
2 teaspoons lemon juice

Mix together ingredients. Add more juice if necessary. Drizzle over cooled peach bread.

Courtesy of South Carolina Peach Council

PEACHY PECAN BREAD

1 cup sugar
¼ cup mayonnaise
2 eggs
1 cup mashed peaches (fresh or canned)
2 cups flour
1 teaspoon cinnamon
1 teaspoon baking powder
1 teaspoon baking soda
¼ teaspoon vanilla extract
1 cup chopped pecans

Preheat oven to 325 degrees. Cream sugar and mayonnaise, add eggs, mixing well. Add mashed peaches and mix well. In a separate bowl, combine dry ingredients and add to creamed mixture. Add vanilla and chopped pecans. Stir until well blended. Pour mixture into a well-greased 8 x 4-inch loaf pan. Bake at 325 degrees for 55 to 60 minutes or until tested done.

Cecelia Drake and Mary Wendzel, Glad Peach Bake Fest Winners, Coloma, Michigan

PEACH TEA BREAD

2½ cups flour

1 cup sugar

1 tablespoon baking powder

½ teaspoon salt

¼ teaspoon nutmeg

1½ cups finely chopped South Carolina peaches,

1 tablespoon lemon juice

⅓ cup oil

⅓ cup milk

2 teaspoon vanilla extract

2 large eggs

⅓ cup finely chopped pecans

Preheat oven to 350 degrees. Spray a 9 x 5-inch loaf pan with cooking spray. In a large bowl, combine flour, sugar, baking powder, salt and nutmeg. In medium size bowl, combine peaches and lemon juice. In another bowl, combine oil, milk, eggs and vanilla. Add oil mixture to flour mixture and stir just until dry ingredients are moistened. Do not over beat. Fold in peaches and nuts. Spoon batter into greased pan. Bake for 55 to 60 minutes or until top is golden brown and center springs back when lightly touched, or test for doneness with a toothpick. Cool in pan on wire rack for 10 minutes. Serve warm.

Courtesy of South Carolina Peach Council

AMARETTO FRUITED BREAD

½ cup Amaretto liquor

¼ cup orange juice

⅔ cup dried peaches, coarsely chopped

⅔ cup dried black mission figs, stems trimmed, coarsely chopped

1 stick unsalted butter, at room temperature

⅔ cup light brown sugar

2 large eggs

1½ cups flour

1 teaspoon baking powder

¼ teaspoon salt

2 tablespoons milk

½ cup coarsely chopped pecans

In a small saucepan, heat Amaretto and orange juice until steaming. Stir in peaches and figs. Set aside for 20 minutes. Preheat oven to 350 degrees. Spray a 9 x 5-inch pan with nonstick cooking spray. With an electric mixer, cream the butter and sugar until fluffy. Beat in the eggs one at a time. Add flour, baking powder, and salt and blend until smooth. Add milk and blend. Strain the liquid from the fruits and add it to the batter. Beat until smooth. Stir in the fruits, followed by nuts. Transfer the batter to the prepared pan. Bake until the top is browned and a toothpick inserted into the center comes out clean, about 50 minutes. Cool the loaf completely before slicing. Can be stored in plastic wrap for up to 5 days at room temperature. GREAT FOR CHRISTMAS BRUNCH!

Courtesy of South Carolina Peach Council

PEACH, PINEAPPLE, ZUCCHINI BREAD

3 eggs
2 cups sugar
1 cup salad oil
2 teaspoons vanilla
1 cup peaches, chopped fine
1 cup shredded zucchini (raw and unpeeled)
1 (8¼-ounce) can crushed pineapple, well drained
2 teaspoons nutmeg
3 cups flour
2 teaspoons baking soda
1 teaspoon salt
1½ teaspoons cinnamon
½ teaspoon baking powder
1 cup chopped nuts

Preheat oven to 350 degrees. Beat together eggs, sugar, oil, and vanilla until thick and foamy. Stir in peaches, zucchini and pineapple. Combine all dry ingredients (except nuts) in a separate bowl and add to peach mixture. Gently fold in nuts. Pour into 2 greased and floured 9 x 3-inch loaf pans. Bake at 350 degrees for 1 hour.

Marianne Page, Glad Peach Bake Fest Winner, Coloma, Michigan

GINGER PEACH PECAN BREAD

2⅓ cups all-purpose flour
⅓ cup sugar
1 cup molasses
¾ cup hot water
½ cup shortening
1 egg
½ cup chopped pecans
1 teaspoon baking soda
1 teaspoon ground ginger
1 teaspoon ground cinnamon
¾ teaspoon salt
1 small can peaches, drained and cut into small pieces

Preheat oven to 350 degrees. Grease and flour a 9 x 9 x 2-inch pan. In a large mixing bowl, combine all ingredients and beat on low speed for 30 seconds, scraping bowl constantly. Beat on medium speed for 3 minutes, scraping bowl occasionally. Pour into prepared pan. Bake until wooden pick inserted into center comes out clean, about 50 minutes.

Ashley Hert, Glad Peach Bake Fest Winner, Coloma, Michigan

PEACH MORNING MUFFINS

2 cups finely chopped fresh South Carolina peaches

1¼ cups sugar, divided

½ cup (1 stick) butter, at room temperature

2 eggs

1½ cups milk

4 cups flour

4 teaspoons baking powder

1 teaspoon salt

¼ cup brown sugar

¼ cup ground pecans

¼ teaspoon ground cinnamon

4 tablespoons cold butter

Preheat oven to 400 degrees. Lightly grease 24 (2 ¾ x 1⅜-inch) muffin cups. Place the peaches in a bowl and cover with ½ cup of the sugar. Mix thoroughly. Allow the peaches to sit for 1 hour. Using an electric mixer, fitted with a paddle, cream the butter and remaining ¾ cup of sugar until smooth and pale in color, about 3 minutes. Add the eggs, one at a time, and beat until fluffy, about 2 minutes. In a mixing bowl, combine 3½ cups of the flour, baking powder, and salt. Remove the bowl from the mixer and alternately fold in the milk and flour mixture, being careful not to over mix. Fold in the peaches. Spoon ¼ cup of the filling into each prepared muffin cup.

In a small bowl, combine the remaining flour, brown sugar, pecans, and cinnamon. Mix well. Add the butter. Using your hands, mix until the mixture resembles coarse crumb like mixture. Sprinkle 1 teaspoon of the crumb mixture over each muffin cup. Bake for about 15 to 20 minutes or until golden brown. Serve warm with butter.

Courtesy of South Carolina Peach Council

SUNRISE CALIFORNIA CLING PEACH MUFFINS

For freshness, store muffins in an airtight container.

2¾ cups all-purpose flour
1 teaspoon baking soda
½ teaspoon salt
1 cup packed brown sugar
¾ cup butter, softened
1 egg
1 cup buttermilk
1 teaspoon vanilla
½ teaspoon finely grated lime peel
1 (15-ounce) can California cling peach slices, drained and cut into small cubes
½ cup shredded sweetened coconut

Preheat oven to 350 degrees. In a large bowl, combine flour, baking soda and salt. In a separate bowl, blend sugar with butter until smooth and light. Whisk in egg, buttermilk, vanilla and lime peel. Pour over dry ingredients. Add peaches and coconut; stir just until dry ingredients are moistened. Spoon batter into lightly oiled or paper-lined muffin cups, filling three-fourths full. Bake on the center rack in preheated oven for 30 to 35 minutes or until tops are firm to the touch. Gently lift from pan and cool on a rack. For a glossy look, brush each muffin, while still warm, with a little honey. Yield: 12 large muffins.

Courtesy of California Cling Peach Board

ISRAELITE HOUSE OF DAVID (1903)
as Reorganized by Mary Purnell, 1930

Many Americans associate this Benton Harbor, Michigan Christian community with the "Jesus Boys" baseball team, a group of long haired athletes who toured the country in the 1920's and 1930's, making a name for themselves with their athletic prowess and their long hair and beards. The history making baseball team was just one of the many contributions this small communal Christian organization made to both their home state of Michigan and to U.S. culture as a whole.

Founded in 1903 by itinerant preachers Benjamin and Mary Purnell, this community of faith still exists today, although it did divide into two separate entities in 1930. Both groups are still active and are located in Benton Harbor. One group is the original Israelite House of David and the other is Mary's City of David (the Israel-ite House of David), as reorganized by Mary Purnell in 1930.

Attracting people from all walks of life, the original membership included over 700 people from all over the world. According to their website, "By the mid 1930's… the Israelite and its reorganization, Mary's City of David, would come to dominate southwestern Michigan's economy, tourism and agricultural industries." Developers of the first pre-Disney theme park and resort, as well as traveling jazz bands, the group also invented the waffle cone and the automatic bowling pin setting machine. One of their founding families was one of America's earliest automobile makers (1894). Another significant contribution was the right to vote that was extended to the women of the community – 17 years before the 19th Amendment to the U.S. Constitution.

From professional athletes to musicians to inventors to scholars, as well as the farmers who tended the hundreds of acres of fruit and vegetable farms, the House of David membership left its mark on the world. Their invention of the first cold storage facility for fruit allowed for the growth of the Benton Harbor Fruit Market, putting the town at the forefront of agricultural development and distribution in its era.

The members of the third oldest American Christian community are gentle people, adhering to the principal that the proving of faith is through work. According to my good friend Ron, (R. James Taylor), in his pictorial history MARY'S CITY OF DAVID, "…faith, courage, determination and long hours of unpretentious

how to price our own for market. I encourage you to meet them by logging on to their website: www.maryscityofdavid.org or by dropping in for a visit if you're passing their way. They have guided tours of their buildings and gardens, offer a working museum and still sponsor baseball games for the House of David Echoes.

sweat…stand behind the original 396 signatures in the Roll Book of Mary's City of David." This remarkable group included craftsmen, carpenters, architects, builders, printers, physicians, vegetarian restaurateurs, musicians, bakers, athletes, skilled tradesmen and writers, as well as traveling preachers.

As a child, I remember going to the House of David amusement park. I entered the weekly talent show where big bands played and I actually won a singing competition. I call this my "15 minutes" of fame!

My family took mirrors to be silvered, tables to be refurnished, farm equipment to be mended and of course we would check their peach prices so we would know

PEACHES AND CREAM MUFFINS

2½   cups all-purpose flour

¼   teaspoon salt

1½   teaspoons baking powder

½   cup butter or margarine, softened

½   cup sugar

1   cup milk

1   large egg

1   cup fresh peaches, peeled and diced

Melted butter

½   cup sliced almonds, toasted lightly

Sugar

PEACH CREAM FILLING:

1   (8-ounce) package cream cheese, softened

1   cup peach preserves, mashed

1   teaspoon vanilla extract

Preheat oven to 375 degrees. Spray a 12-cup muffin tin. In a mixing bowl, combine flour, salt and baking powder. Set aside. In a large bowl, cream together butter and sugar. In a separate bowl, beat milk and eggs together. Add to creamed mixture, blending lightly. Add dry ingredients to creamed mixture, blending well. Fold in diced peaches. Fill muffin cups with batter about two-thirds full. Bake for 20–25 minutes. Five minutes or so after removing muffins from oven brush with melted butter. Gently press a few toasted almonds on top of each muffin and sprinkle with sugar.

After muffins have completely cooled, cream the filling ingredients together. Place in pastry bag with a large mouth tip and gently squeeze peach cream into each muffin by inserting the tip into the middle of the bottom of each muffin. Gently squeeze, do not over fill. Store in refrigerator until ready to serve. Take muffins out of refrigerator about 10–15 minutes before serving to allow cream mixture to soften.

Susan Zeilenga, Glad Peach Bake Fest Winner, Coloma, Michigan

PEACHY MUFFINS

2 cups Bisquick® Mix
⅔ cup milk
1 egg
1 tablespoon vanilla extract
1 cup peaches (pealed, cut, and finely mixed with a mixer)
¼ cup sugar

Preheat oven to 450 degrees. Combine all ingredients in a bowl. Mix well. If too doughy, add a little more milk, not too much, you don't want it runny. Fill muffin tin cups half full. Bake 10-12 minutes in preheated oven until browned. If you like, you can sprinkle muffin batter with sugar before baking.

Deb Hemenway, Glad Peach Bake Fest Winner, Coloma, Michigan

SEASON 1933

SHAFER FARMS

Visual interest satisfies some customers but Tom and Wendy Shafer have continued to encourage the emotional connection of good quality and taste that Shafer orchards have been known for since 1936. Chicago clients are their largest customer base formerly it was the Europeans and now it is the Spanish.

PEACHY LEMON POPPY MUFFINS

1 teaspoon baking soda
⅔ cup pureed peaches
10 tablespoons butter, softened
1 cup sugar
2 eggs
1¼ cups flour
¼ teaspoon salt
½ teaspoon vanilla extract
3 tablespoons poppy seeds
⅓ cup lemon juice
1 tablespoon yellow food coloring

Preheat oven to 350 degrees. Grease a 12-cup muffin tin. Stir baking soda into pureed peaches, set aside. They will foam. Cream butter and sugar together, add eggs, one at a time. Alternately add flour and peaches. Then add salt, vanilla, poppy seeds, lemon juice, and food coloring, mix until blended. Fill muffin cups nearly to top. Bake for 20–25 minutes in preheated 350 degree oven.

Jacquelyn Hert and Mary Harrell, Glad Peach Bake Fest Winners, Coloma, Michigan

GEORGIA PEACH RASPBERRY MELBA MUFFINS

1 cup diced fresh Georgia peaches
½ teaspoon cinnamon
2 cups all-purpose flour
½ cup sugar
2½ teaspoons baking powder
½ teaspoon salt
½ cup chopped walnuts
1 egg
1 cup milk
⅓ cup butter, melted
2 tablespoons brandy
Raspberry jam

Preheat oven to 400 degrees. In a bowl, sprinkle peaches with cinnamon and set aside. In a separate bowl, sift together flour, sugar, baking powder and salt; stir in walnuts. In a separate bowl, whisk egg, milk, butter and brandy together and stir into peaches. Make a "well" in the dry ingredients and fill with peach mixture. Mix lightly, just until moistened. Fill 12 greased muffin cups half full; place 1 teaspoon of raspberry jam in the center of each; cover with batter until two-thirds full. Bake at 400 degrees for 20 to 25 minutes until golden brown. Yield: 12 muffins.

Courtesy of Dickey Farms, Musella, Georgia, "The Sweetest Peaches in the South"

PEACHES AND CREAM CINNAMON ROLLS

1 (26.4-ounce) package frozen biscuits
1 (6-ounce) package dried peaches
All-purpose flour
½ (8-ounce) package softened cream cheese
¼ cup firmly packed brown sugar
1 teaspoon ground cinnamon
1 cup confectioners' sugar
3 tablespoons milk
½ teaspoon pure vanilla extract

GLAZE

1 cup confectioners' sugar
3 tablespoons milk
½ teaspoon vanilla

Preheat oven to 375 degrees. Coat a 12 serving 3-inch muffin pan with nonstick spray and place muffin cups in each cavity. Arrange frozen biscuits, with sides touching, in 3 rows of 4 biscuits on a lightly floured surface. Let stand for 30 minutes or until biscuits are thawed but still cool to the touch. Pour boiling water to cover over dried peaches, and let stand 10 minutes; drain well. Chop peaches. Sprinkle biscuits lightly with flour. Press biscuit edges together, and pat to form a 10 x 12-inch rectangle of dough; spread evenly with softened cream cheese. Stir together brown sugar and cinnamon; sprinkle over cream cheese. Sprinkle chopped peaches and pecans evenly over brown sugar mixture. Roll up, starting at one long end; cut into 12 (about 1-inch thick) slices. Place one slice into each muffin cup. Bake at 375 degrees for 20 to 25 minutes or until golden brown. Cool slightly and remove from pan.

Stir all glaze ingredients together. Drizzle evenly over rolls. Makes 1 dozen.

Courtesy of South Carolina Peach Council

PEACH SWIRL BREAKFAST ROLLS

1 can refrigerated crescent rolls
2 tablespoons melted butter
2 heaping tablespoons sour cream
Peach jam or marmalade
¼ cup chopped nuts (pecans or walnuts)
¼ cup flaked coconut
¼ teaspoon cinnamon

PEACH GLAZE

1 cup sifted confectioners' sugar
1½ tablespoons fresh peach puree

Preheat oven to 450 degrees. Spread rolls out on lightly floured board and work them into a rectangle about ¼-inch thick. (Do not separate rolls). Brush with melted butter. Spread on sour cream and then spread on jam or marmalade. Sprinkle with nuts and coconut. Sprinkle on a small amount of cinnamon. Roll up jelly roll fashion beginning with the long side of the dough. Cut into 9 equal slices. Place swirls in buttered dish or baking sheet, cut side down. Dot lightly with butter, if desired. Bake at 450 degrees for 20 minutes.

Peach Glaze: mix confectioners' sugar with fresh peach puree until smooth. Drizzle over baked swirls. Top with any left over chopped pecans if desired.

Brenda McCuan, Glad Peach Bake Fest Winner, Coloma, Michigan

PEACH CINNAMON ROLLS

DOUGH

1 cup milk, scalded
¼ cup sugar
¼ cup shortening
1 teaspoon salt
3½ cups self-rising flour
1 egg

FILLING

½ cup sugar
½ cup butter, melted
2 cups peach chunks
2 tablespoons cinnamon
1 cup raisins

TOPPING

1 can cream cheese frosting

Combine in a bowl scalded milk, sugar, shortening, salt, flour and egg. Mix well then roll out on a flat floured surface into an 8 x 16-inch rectangle. Sprinkle all filling ingredients over dough. Roll dough and filling ingredients up in a jelly roll shape. Cut roll into 1½-inch slices, lay on ungreased cookie sheet, then bake at 375 degrees for about 20 minutes. Cool and frost with cream cheese frosting.

Debra Pena, Glad Peach Bake Fest Winner, Coloma, Michigan

PEACHY BLUE NUT BREAD ROLLS

1 loaf frozen white bread dough
1 (5-ounce) package solo nut filling paste
1 medium can sliced peaches in heavy syrup
3 teaspoons cinnamon
Cornstarch (just a little to thicken syrup)
Chopped pecans
1 (16-ounce) can blueberry pie filling
2½ tablespoons cornstarch
2 ounces water
⅛ cup peach flavoring

Preheat oven to 350 degrees. Thaw bread dough, let rise and punch down dough until flat. Spread nut filling in center of bread but not all the way to the edges. Cook peaches, cinnamon and cornstarch until thickened. Roll dough in a jelly roll fashion. Slice ½-inch thick then place slices onto a well greased sheet pan. Bake in a 350 degree oven for 20 minutes. Brush with real butter right away, cool slightly. Cook blueberry filling, cornstarch, water and peach flavoring until warm. Spoon over rolls and serve.

Renee McCream, Glad Peach Bake Fest Winner, Coloma, Michigan

FRUIT ACRES
Farm Market & U-Pick

Randy and Annette Friday Bjorge's ancestors immigrated to the United States from Germany in 1846. Fruit Acres Farms is the 230 acre farm that they founded and it is still thriving today, under the guidance of fifth generation family members. For many years, the farm was the site of the annual Blessing of the Blossoms held during Blossom Week held in May. Peaches in their orchard are hand cross-pollinated on a mother tree just as farmers have done for hundreds of years.

A visit to the farm during the summer includes strawberries in June, wagon rides, play areas for the kids, a vegetable and flower market, pick your own apples from dwarf trees (no ladders to worry with), a pumpkin patch in September and October, and of course – peaches in July and August. Visit their web site: http://www.fruitacresfarms.com/index.htm for directions and dates of operation. The site includes the expected harvest date for a variety of peaches, so you can plan to pick your favorites at just the right time.

PEACH OATMEAL COFFEE CAKE

OAT-STREUSEL TOPPING

2 tablespoons firm stick margarine or butter
2 tablespoons packed brown sugar
¼ cup quick cooking or old fashioned oats
¼ cup all purpose flour
½ teaspoon ground cinnamon

COFFEE CAKE

1¾ cups flour
¾ cup oats
1 cup buttermilk
1 teaspoon cinnamon
1 egg
1 cup packed brown sugar
½ cup stick margarine, softened
3 teaspoons baking powder
½ teaspoon baking soda
¼ teaspoon ground nutmeg
1½ cups chopped peaches

Preheat oven to 350 degrees. Grease bottom and sides of 9-inch square pan with shortening. Prepare oat streusel topping, set aside. Beat remaining ingredients except peaches in large bowl with electric mixer on low speed for 30 seconds. Beat on medium speed 2 minutes, scraping bowl occasionally. Stir in peaches. Spread batter in pan. Sprinkle with topping. Bake 50–55 minutes or until golden brown and toothpick inserted in center comes out clean. Cool on wire rack or serve warm.

Amanda Perry and Edith Munchow, Glad Peach Bake Fest Winners, Coloma, Michigan

PEACHY PECAN COFFEE CAKE

¾ cup chopped pecans

1 (16-ounce) can sliced peaches in syrup

1 (8-ounce) package cream cheese, softened

1 cup packed light brown sugar

4 large eggs

½ cup half and half

1½ teaspoons almond extract

1 cup ginger snap cookie crumbs

1 (6-ounce) package almond brickle chips

½ cup flaked coconut

Whipped cream, optional

Preheat oven to 350 degrees. Lightly grease a 9-inch square pan. Set aside. Spread pecans in a single layer on an ungreased baking sheet. Bake pecans until lightly browned, about 10–12 minutes, stirring occasionally. Drain peaches well, discard syrup or save for another use. Chop drained peaches and set aside. Beat softened cream cheese and brown sugar in a large bowl until mixture is well blended. Add eggs, one at a time, beating well after each addition. Blend in half and half and almond extract. Stir in ginger snap cookie crumbs, brickle chips, toasted pecans, and coconut flakes. Stir in chopped peaches, spread in prepared baking pan. Bake cake until center is firm and edges are golden, about 35–40 minutes. Serve with whipped cream, if desired.

Brenda McCuan, Glad Peach Bake Fest Winner, Coloma, Michigan

GEORGIA PEACH SOUR CREAM COFFEE CAKE

STREUSEL TOPPING/FILLING

2 cups chopped pecans

3 tablespoons sugar

⅓ cup packed brown sugar

1 teaspoon ground cinnamon

CAKE

½ cup butter-flavored shortening

1 cup sugar

2 eggs

2 cups all-purpose flour

1½ teaspoons baking powder

½ teaspoon baking soda

½ teaspoon salt

2 cups sliced peeled fresh Georgia peaches

1 cup sour cream

1 teaspoon vanilla extract

Preheat oven to 350 degrees. Combine all streusel ingredients; set aside. In a large mixing bowl, cream shortening and sugar until fluffy. Beat in eggs.

Combine all dry ingredients; add alternately with the sour cream and vanilla to the creamed mixture. Beat until smooth. Pour half the batter into a 9-inch spring form pan. Sprinkle with 1 cup of the streusel. Top with remaining batter and half-cup cup streusel. Bake at 350 degrees for 30 minutes. Arrange peaches over cake; sprinkle with remaining streusel. Bake an additional 30 to 40 minutes or until cake tests done. Cool cake 10 minutes before removing sides of pan. Serve warm or at room temperature. Yield: 12 servings.

(Opposite) Land of the giants – Paul Friday breaks his own record for the world's largest peach – 11 times. Peaches were from the same tree, with the biggest weighing 30.5 ounces. This surpassed Paul's previous 25.6 ounce peach, which was listed in the Guinness Book of Records. Pictured are Paul Friday, his assistant Jerry Nolasco, and Benton Fruit Market Manager, Lee LaVanway. AUTHOR'S NOTE: The mighty have fallen – sort of. In 2007 Paul's record was broken by Bill and Andy Schultz. They produced a 30.9 ounce peach, breaking the record by .2 ounce. The variety was one of Paul's own – Friday's Flamin' Fury No. PF-24-007, so in a sense, Paul beat himself! And he still wins!
© *Courtesy of the Herald Palladium and Michael Eliasohn.*

PEACHES AND CREAM COFFEE CAKE

CRUST:

- 1½–2 cups all purpose flour, divided
- 2 tablespoons sugar
- 2 tablespoons butter or margarine, softened
- ½ teaspoon salt
- 1 package quick acting dry yeast
- ⅔ cup water, 120–130 degrees

CREAM CHEESE FILLING:

- 12 ounces cream cheese, softened
- ½ teaspoon ground nutmeg
- ¼ cup sugar
- 1 teaspoon vanilla extract

PEACHES:

- 2 (15-ounce) cans peaches, thinly sliced

STREUSEL TOPPING:

- 1 tablespoon firm butter
- 3 tablespoons brown sugar
- 3 tablespoons flour
- 1 teaspoon cinnamon

GLAZE (OPTIONAL):

- ½ cup confectioners' sugar
- 1½ teaspoons hot water
- ¼ teaspoon vanilla extract

Crust: Combine ¾ cup flour, sugar, butter, salt, and yeast in large bowl. Add water and mix till dough pulls away from bowl. (Dough will be sticky). Using floured fingers, pat dough onto greased parchment paper lined jelly roll pan. Cover and let rest 15 minutes. Preheat oven to 350 degrees. Bake crust for approximately 5 minutes.

To assemble: Prepare cream cheese filling by beating all ingredients till smooth. Spread evenly over crust. Then add a layer of thinly sliced peaches. Then layer streusel topping over cake. Bake 20–25 minutes or until crust is a light golden brown.

Optional glaze: Mix glaze ingredients until a drizzling consistency. Once cake is cooled, top with glaze.

Renee Johnson, Glad Peach Bake Fest Winner, Coloma, Michigan

PEACH COFFEE CAKE

1 (20-ounce) can crushed pineapple, with its own juice
2 bags frozen peaches
1 box white cake mix
Walnuts
Raisins
Brown sugar
1 stick butter, melted

Preheat oven to 350 degrees. Spray a 13 x 9-inch pan with non-stick cooking spray. Spread crushed pineapple and juice in bottom of pan. Place one bag of peaches over pineapple. Sprinkle cake mix over peaches and top with walnuts and raisins, if desired. Place second bag of peaches over nut/raisin mixture. Top with a mixture of brown sugar, raisins and walnuts. Pour melted butter over top. Bake in preheated oven for 1 hour.

Jeri Skjordal, Glad Peach Bake Fest Winner, Coloma, Michigan

KRISPY KREME® PEACH COFFEE CAKE

2 dozen glazed Krispy Kreme® donuts
2 eggs, well beaten
1 can sweetened condensed milk
1 can diced peaches, with juice
Pinch of salt
1 teaspoon cinnamon
½ cup golden raisins

TOPPING:

1 stick butter, melted
1 pound confectioners' sugar
1 teaspoon almond flavor

Preheat oven to 350 degrees. In a very large bowl, cut each donut into 8 pieces. In a separate bowl, beat eggs well and pour evenly over donuts. Pour condensed milk over donuts. Add diced peaches and juice to donut mixture. Add salt, cinnamon and raisins to donut mixture. Mix well. Coat a 13 x 9-inch pan with non-stick cooking spray. Pour mixture into pan. It will be very full, but will settle when cooked. Bake in preheated 350 degree oven for 45 minutes or until done in middle. Mix together topping ingredients and drizzle over top of hot cake. Cut into squares and serve.

Brenda McCuan, Glad Peach Bake Fest Winner, Coloma, Michigan

PEACH POPOVER PANCAKES

Makes one large pancake that will serve 6 to 8.

¼ cup butter, softened
1 pound South Carolina peaches, cut into thin slices (about 2 cups)
¾ cup sugar
1¼ cups all-purpose flour
1¼ cups skim milk
2 eggs or ½ cup fat free egg substitute
2 teaspoons baking powder

Preheat oven to 375 degrees. Put the butter into a deep 2– 3-quart casserole dish and place in the oven. Toss the peach slices in a bowl with ¼ cup of the sugar. Set aside. Place the remaining ½ cup sugar, flour, milk, eggs, and baking powder in a blender and liquefy. Or place in a medium bowl and work with an electric beater until the batter is smooth. When the butter has melted to a sizzling point, about 3 to 5 minutes, remove the hot dish from the oven. Immediately pour the batter into the dish and spoon the sugared peaches and juice on top. Return to the oven and bake for 50 minutes, or until the pancake has risen and is golden brown. Serve warm.

Courtesy of South Carolina Peach Council

Cakes, Cookies & Bars

PEACH ANGEL FOOD TUNNEL CAKE

1 (20-ounce) prepared angel food cake or your favorite scratch recipe

¾ cup sliced natural almonds

1 (8-ounce) tub Cool Whip® with ½ teaspoon almond extract added

6 peaches, pitted, peeled and coarsely chopped

Place cake on a platter. In skillet over medium heat, cook almonds, stirring frequently until roasted, 1–2 minutes. Blend Cool Whip® and almond extract. Transfer 1½ cups to a separate bowl and fold in chopped peaches. Set aside.

Cut 1-inch horizontal layer from top of cake and set aside. Using small knife, cut tunnel in cake ½-inch from inside and outside edges, pull out cake from center, reserve cake pieces for another use. Fill tunnel with reserved peach-Cool Whip® mixture. Replace top of cake cover with remaining Cool Whip®, press toasted almonds into sides of cake. Garnish with peaches and mix if desired.

If peaches are used to decorate the top of the cake, be sure to rub each slice with lemon juice to keep them from turning brown. May be stored in freezer.

Barbara Adams, Glad Peach Bake Fest Winner, Coloma, Michigan

PEACH FILLING

1 cup beaten cream

1 cup confectioners' sugar

1 cup peach pulp

2 tablespoons lemon juice

Few grains salt

Mix ingredients, spread between two baked layers of prepared 8 or 9-inch white or yellow cake.

AUNTIE'S DRIED PEACH CAKE

1 cup dried peaches
2¼ cups sugar, divided
1 cup vegetable oil
4 eggs
1 teaspoon nutmeg
1 teaspoon cinnamon
1 teaspoon baking soda
1 teaspoon salt
2 cups flour
1 cup buttermilk
1 cup chopped pecans (optional)

Preheat oven to 350 degrees. Place peaches in a small saucepan. Cover with water. Add ¼ cup sugar. Cook until tender. Mash and set aside.

Mix oil and 2 cups sugar. Add eggs, one at a time. In a separate bowl, combine dry ingredients. Add flour mixture alternately with buttermilk to sugar mixture. Mix well. Fold in mashed peaches and pecans (if desired). Bake in a 13 x 9-inch pan at 350 degrees for 45 minutes. Pour sauce over top.

SAUCE

1 cup sugar
¼ cup margarine
½ cup buttermilk
½ teaspoon baking soda

Combine ingredients in large saucepan. Bring to full boil for 2 minutes, stirring constantly. Pour over hot cake.

Thanks to Martha Lewis, Canton, Texas

DRIED PEACH CAKE WITH WHITE CHOCOLATE FROSTING

2 (8-inch) cake layers (box is fine —prepare according to directions on box)

PEACH FILLING

12 ounces dried peaches
⅔ cup sugar
1 tablespoon cornstarch
¾ cup water
2 tablespoons orange juice
1 tablespoon peach brandy
1 tablespoon butter
2 egg yolks, lightly beaten

FROSTING

11 ounces white chocolate, finely chopped
12 ounces cream cheese, room temperature
¾ cup butter, room temperature
2 tablespoons lemon juice

Peach Filling: Process peaches and sugar until finely chopped. Combine peach mixture, cornstarch, water, orange juice, brandy and butter in a sauce pan. Bring to a boil over medium heat and cook, stirring constantly for 3 to 4 minutes. Gradually stir one-fourth of hot mixture into eggs. Add egg mixture to remaining hot mixture, stirring constantly for 1 minute. Cool filling and chill for 1 hour.

Frosting: In a double boiler, melt white chocolate over simmering water until almost melted. Remove from water and stir until smooth. Let cool. In a separate bowl, beat cream cheese and butter until smooth. Add lemon juice, mix well. Add cooled white chocolate.

To assemble cake: Place one cake layer, flat side up on serving plate. Build a small ridge with frosting around the edge using a spoon, piping bag or a small baggie with a small notch cut out of one corner. Place half of the peach filling on the first layer. Place second layer, round side up, on top of the first layer. Frost cake, leaving top plain. Again, make a small ridge around the edge of top layer, fill in the rest of the filling.

Vera Schuhjnecht, Glad Peach Bake Fest Winner, Coloma, Michigan

PEACHY NUT CAKE

1 (28-ounce) can peaches
1 box butter pecan cake mix
¾ cup butter, melted
½ cup chopped nuts

Preheat oven to 325 degrees. Place peaches into a 13 x 9 x 2-inch pan. Evenly sprinkle cake mix over peaches. Pour melted butter over mixture. Add nuts. Bake in preheated 325 degree oven for 55 minutes.

Sharon McFall, Busy Woman's Cookbook©

Caramel or Burn

sugar and 1 cup hot water,
caramel sirup.
butter or other fat.
ps sugar.

brown the cup of sug
t water, cook until a
gar together, add th
ry ingredients, add
ablespoons of the ca
: in greased muffin p
tes and ice with ca

Quick C

d flour.
baking powder.
s sugar.
salt.
butter or other fat

the flour, baking
our to mix with
the milk and flo
l it is about 1½
erate oven (350
mixture of the
the oven again
t or cold.

Devil'

¼ cup butter or other fat.
1 cup sugar.
2 eggs.
1¾ cups sifted soft-wheat flour.
2 teaspoons baking powder.

Cream the butter and the su
well. Sift together the flour, b
first mixture alternately with th
and add with the vanilla to the
in a shallow greased pan in a ver
minutes. Just before serving c
if preferred, bake the cake in tw
In this cake sour milk may be
add one-half teaspoon soda to th
also be increased by 1 square, i

d Crumb Cake

¼ teaspoon cinnamon.
¼ teaspoon salt.
y dry
¼ teaspoon almond extract.
1 teaspoon vanilla.

gar, and stir in the other ingredients. Pat
allow greased pan, bake in a very moderate
minutes. This has somewhat the texture
is a good way to use up stale bread.

. S. Department of Agriculture, gives recipes for the standard ways

JOE SAGE

On the picturesque, hilly Schumel Road in Hagar Township, Michigan you experience a small farm owned by Joe Sage in cooperation with his daughter Laurie and son Donald. The farm started in 1925 and some of the family were former members of The House of David.

PEACHY COLADA CAKE

    1 package white cake mix
    1 cup flaked coconut
    1 small package coconut instant pudding
    ¼ cup vegetable oil
    4 eggs
    1¼ cups water
    ⅓ cup Malibu Rum

FROSTING

    1 (20-ounce) can peaches, divided
    1 (8-ounce) tub Cool Whip®
    1 small package vanilla instant pudding
    ⅓ cup Malibu Rum

Preheat oven to 350 degrees. Mix all cake ingredients together. Pour into two 8-inch greased cake pans. Bake in preheated oven for 30 minutes. Let cool. To prepare frosting: Crush 1 cup canned peaches then combine with Cool Whip®, rum and pudding. Dice up ½ cup canned peaches, set aside. Frost first layer of cake, place diced peaches on top. Place second layer of cake on top of first layer. Frost. Decorate cake with remaining peaches. Cover cake and place in refrigerator.

Lisa Heaton, Glad Peach Bake Fest Winner, Coloma, Michigan

BUTTER BRICKLE PEACH CAKE

    4 large ripe peaches
    1 stick margarine, melted
    1 box Butter Brickle cake mix

Preheat oven to 350 degrees. Coat the bottom of a 13 x 9-inch baking pan with non-stick vegetable spray, or use solid vegetable shortening or margarine. Peel peaches and slice thin. Save juice. Combine peaches, melted margarine and cake mix and pour into prepared pan. Bake for about 45 minutes in preheated oven. Serves 12.

Elbertas in orchard of Hon. C.J. Monroe, South Haven, Michigan. Photo Courtesy Dr. Paul Rood and the State Horticultural Society of Michigan.

PEACH SPICE CAKE

2 cups sugar

1 cup vegetable oil

2 eggs

4 cups all-purpose flour

2 teaspoons baking soda

1 teaspoon salt

1 teaspoon nutmeg

1 teaspoon cloves

1 teaspoon allspice

1 teaspoon cinnamon

1 (20-ounce) can sliced peaches with juice

1 cup chopped nuts

Preheat oven to 375 degrees. Cream sugar and oil until light. Add eggs, one at a time, beating after each addition. Sift flour before measuring. Sift dry ingredients together. Add to creamed mixture with peaches. Stir in nuts. Turn into greased and lightly floured 10-inch tube pan. Bake at 375 degrees for 1 hour and 20 minutes. Invert pan on rack and cool.

Thanks to Polly Godfrey, Eva, Oklahoma and Linda Martin, Athens, Texas, Keep Your Fork Cookbook ©

PEACH CAKE

½ cup packed brown sugar

1 cup sugar

1 cup self rising flour

¾ stick butter or margarine

2 eggs

½ cup milk

2 teaspoons vanilla extract

3 cups fresh peaches

Preheat oven to 325 degrees. Mix all dry ingredients together well. In a separate bowl, combine margarine, eggs, milk and vanilla extract. Combine dry and wet ingredients together to form cake batter. Coat a 13 x 9-inch pan with non-stick cooking spray. Layer peaches and batter until all ingredients are used. Bake at 325 degrees for 35–40 minutes or until golden brown. Serve cold with whipped cream or Cool Whip®.

Marie Taylor, Glad Peach Bake Fest Winner, Coloma, Michigan

HOTSPOT'S PEACHY PASSION

1 box yellow cake mix

1 stick butter

2 cups peaches, drained (can be canned or frozen)

1 (8-ounce) carton sour cream

½ cup packed brown sugar

½ teaspoon cinnamon

1 (12-ounce) tub frozen whipped topping

Preheat oven to 350 degrees. Mix cake mix and butter and press into a 13 x 9-inch pan. Combine peaches, sour cream, brown sugar and cinnamon together and pour over cake mixture. Bake in preheated oven for 40 minutes. Cool and serve topped with whipped topping. Serve cold.

Violet Jewell, Glad Peach Bake Fest Winner, Coloma, Michigan

PEACHY VANILLA WAFER CAKE

1 cup butter, softened (2 sticks)

2 cups sugar

6 large eggs

1 cup diced peaches, do not drain

7 ounces shredded coconut

1 (12-ounce) package vanilla wafers, finely crushed

Preheat oven to 275 degrees. Grease a 13 x 9-inch (or tube) pan and line bottom with waxed paper. Combine butter and sugar in a large bowl. Beat with an electric mixer set at high speed until mixture is light and fluffy. Add eggs, one at a time, beating well after each addition. Stir in peaches and coconut. Add vanilla wafer crumbs and mix well. Spoon cake batter into the prepared pan. Bake cake for 1 hour and 45 minutes or until a toothpick inserted into center comes out clean. Cool in pan for 10 minutes, turn out onto plate. Top with Cool Whip®, if desired.

Brenda McCuan, Glad Peach Bake Fest Winner, Coloma, Michigan

PEACH CAKE

1 stick butter	3 teaspoons baking powder
1½ cups sugar	¼ cup oil
2 eggs, separated	2 cups milk
4 cups flour	2 teaspoons almond extract

Mix and add egg whites, beaten stiff. Oil and flour a 10 x 15-inch baking pan and pour above mixture. On top, place sliced peaches and cover with "streusel" crumbs.

TOPPING

2 eggs, separated	1 cup milk
¾ cup sugar	Sour cream/yogurt/ cream cheese
4 tablespoons flour	Almond or vanilla extract

Mix all and add egg whites, beaten stiff

STREUSEL

3 tablespoons butter	⅓ cup sugar
¾ cup flour	1 teaspoon almond extract

Bake at 350 degrees until brown around the edges. Can be made also with apricots or plums. If using apples, substitute almond extract with vanilla extract.

Thanks to Erika B. Spittzke

PEACH SHORTCAKE

3 cups sifted flour

1 teaspoon salt

3 teaspoons double-acting baking powder

½ cup butter or solid vegetable shortening

¾ cup milk

Butter

1½ quarts sliced peaches, sweetened

Preheat oven to 450 degrees. Sift flour once and then measure. Add salt and baking powder. Sift again. Cut in shortening; add milk all at once and stir carefully until all flour is dampened. Continue to stir vigorously until mixture forms a soft dough and follows the spoon around the bowl. Turn out immediately onto a slightly floured board and knead for 30 seconds. Roll to ¼-inch thickness. Place half of the dough into an ungreased round cake pan; brush with melted butter. Place remaining half on top and brush with melted butter. Bake in preheated 450 degree oven for 15 to 20 minutes. Remove from oven. Separate dough halves and spread bottom half with soft butter and some of the peaches. Place the other half of dough on top and spread with butter and remaining peaches. Garnish with whipped cream. Cut into individual servings. Serves 8.

Note: Other fresh fruits may be substituted for peaches

PEACHES AND CREAM SHORTCAKE

1 package Pillsbury Plus® yellow cake mix
1 (3-ounce) package peach gelatin
⅓ cup water
1 (8-ounce) carton vanilla or peach yogurt
3 eggs
1 cup water
1 (4-ounce) carton Cool Whip®
Peach slices (for garnish)

Preheat oven to 350 degrees. Grease a 13 x 9 x 2-inch pan. Set aside. In a large bowl, combine cake mix, 2 tablespoons of the gelatin, water, yogurt and eggs. Beat at low speed until moistened. Beat 2 minutes at high speed. Pour into prepared pan. Bake at 350 degrees for 30 to 40 minutes or until toothpick inserted in center comes out clean. Cool cake in pan on rack for 15 minutes.

In small saucepan, heat 1 cup water. Add remaining gelatin; stir to dissolve. Using a long-tined fork, pierce cake at ½-inch intervals. Pour gelatin mixture evenly over cake; refrigerate. Serve with whipped topping and sliced peaches. Makes 12 servings.

Thanks to Noreen Soos, Baroda, Michigan

PEACH CAKE ROLL

1 cup less 2 tablespoons all purpose flour
1 teaspoon baking powder
¼ teaspoon salt
3 eggs
1 cup sugar
½ cup water
1 teaspoon vanilla extract
Peach filling
Confectioners' sugar

PEACH FILLING

8 ounces cream cheese
½ cup confectioners' sugar
⅛ teaspoon almond flavoring
1 cup finely diced peaches.

Preheat oven to 350 degrees. Mix together flour, baking powder, and salt. In another bowl, beat eggs 5 minutes or until thick and lemon colored (See note.). Gradually beat in sugar. On low speed gradually blend in water and vanilla. Gradually add dry ingredients, beating just until batter is smooth. Line a 15 x 10 x 1-inch jelly roll with waxed paper, and lightly grease the paper. Pour batter into pan and spread evenly. Bake at 375 degrees for 12–15 minutes or until toothpick inserted in center comes out clean. Remove cake from oven and loosen edges. Invert pan onto a clean towel that has been dusted heavily with confectioners' sugar. Remove waxed paper. While cake is still hot, roll the cake and towel together from the narrow end. Cool on wire rack. When cool, unroll cake and spread with peach filling. Carefully roll cake again and sprinkle outside with confectioners' sugar. Cover and chill thoroughly. Cake can be decorated with confectioners' sugar glaze made with peach juice and top with thin slices of peaches of top. Chill. Yield: 8-10 servings.

Note: Eggs must be beaten for a full 5 minutes and cake must be rolled while still hot.

Peach Filling: Beat cream cheese until smooth and fluffy. Add confectioners' sugar and flavoring; beat until smooth. Mix in diced peaches.

Brenda McCuan, Glad Peach Bake Fest Winner, Coloma, Michigan

GEORGIA PEACHES AND CREAM ROLL

3 eggs
¼ teaspoon salt
¼ teaspoon vanilla
¾ cup sugar
¾ cup complete buttermilk pancake mix
Confectioners' sugar
1 tablespoon light or dark rum
4 large Georgia peaches, peeled and chopped (4 cups)
1 cup whipping cream
½ cup sugar

Preheat oven to 400 degrees. Beat eggs, salt, and vanilla in a large mixing bowl with an electric mixer on high speed about 4 minutes or until thick. Gradually add the ¾ cup sugar; beat on medium speed for 4 to 5 minutes or until light and fluffy. Add pancake mix; beat on low speed just until combined. Spread batter in a greased and floured 15 x 10 x 1-inch baking pan. Bake in a 400 degree oven for 8 to 10 minutes or until golden and cake springs back when lightly touched near center. Immediately loosen edges of cake from pan and turn cake out onto a towel sprinkled with confectioners' sugar. Roll up towel and cake into a spiral, starting from one of the short sides. Cool on a wire rack.

Meanwhile, add rum to peaches; set aside. Beat together whipping cream and the ½ cup sugar until stiff peaks form. Unroll cake; remove towel. Drain peaches. Spread cake with half of the whipped cream; top with drained peaches. Spread with remaining whipped cream. Roll up cake. Place seam side down on a serving platter. If desired, sprinkle with confectioners' sugar. Cover and chill up to 2 hours. Transport in an insulated cooler with ice packs. To serve, cut into 1-inch thick slices. Yield: 10 servings.

Courtesy of Dickey Farms, Musella, Georgia, "The Sweetest Peaches in the South"

PEACH CUSTARD CAKE

Preheat oven to 375 degrees. Put into a bowl 1½ cups butter ???(this is missing something)???and ½ teaspoon salt. Mix with pastry blender until mixture looks like coarse meal. With back of spoon, press mixture firmly into bottom and half way up sides of a buttered 8-inch pan. Drain large can of sliced peaches, saving ½ cup syrup. Arrange peaches on crust in pan. Sprinkle with a mixture of ½ cup sugar and ½ teaspoon cinnamon. Bake 20 minutes. Mix reserved syrup, 1 cup milk and 1 eggs, slightly beaten. Pour over peaches. Bake 30 minutes more or until custard is firm, except in center. Center becomes firm upon standing. Serve warm or cold.
Yield: 9 servings.

Thanks to Mrs. Mona Duer, Hooker, Oklahoma

PEACH KUCHEN

1 cup flour
¼ cup sugar
1 teaspoon baking powder
⅓ cup shortening
¼ cup milk
1 egg

TOPPING

4 cups fruit (peaches)
¾ cup sugar
¼ cup flour
½ teaspoon cinnamon
4 tablespoons butter, melted

Mix together flour, sugar, and baking powder, then add shortening, milk and egg. Mix well. Pour mix into a greased 8 x 8 inch square pan. Arrange sliced peaches over batter, (?)h combine sugar, flour and cinnamon and sprinkle over peaches, then top with melted butter. Bake at 350 degrees for 40 minutes.

Wanda Zurek, Glad Peach Bake Fest Winner, Coloma, Michigan

ROOD FAMILY

In 1870 Edward A. Rood started a farm in Covert, Michigan which is now owned by Paul J. Jr. and Geraldine Rood. The farm's major variety is Sun Haven. They also grow other types of fruit. Their primary customer is the Amish Community; Paul is truly a gentle-man. He and Geraldine continue to live in the beautiful old home which they opened to me along with their hearts. I gleaned so much history as we visited and could view the orchards from the window in early spring.

ROOD FAMILY

The man in center of photo is Alfred Packard, Paul Rood's great uncle, a lumberman and farmer in Covert Township, Michigan. He had his own sawmill to clear the land and later plant peaches.

Men busy digging marl from a creek bed in Barry County, Michigan 1930s. A sign nearby read "Marl-- 25cents a yard-loaded" Picture taken by Frank Rood, County agricultural Agent.

Lamson and Rood packing shed was on a railroad sidetrack in Covert, Michigan. Frank Rood, grandfather of Paul Rood, is foreground, left.

PEACH DELIGHT BUNDT CAKE

Kinda good!!!

    1 cup chopped frozen peach slices (thawed
       and drained)
    ¼ cup packed brown sugar
    2 teaspoons cornstarch
    ¼ teaspoon nutmeg
    1 box yellow or vanilla cake mix
 1¼   cups water
    ⅓ cup butter, softened
    2 eggs

Preheat oven to 325 degrees. Grease and flour a 10–12 cup bundt pan. Set aside. In a medium bowl, stir together peaches, brown sugar, cornstarch, and nutmeg. Mix well. Set aside. In a large bowl, combine cake mix, water, butter, and eggs. Mix on medium speed for 2 minutes. Stir in peach mixture. Spoon into prepared pan. Bake at 325 degrees for 50–60 minutes or until toothpick inserted comes out clean. Cool 10 minutes in pan. Remove from pan. Cool on rack. Sprinkle with confectioners' sugar.

Thanks to Elaine Jensen, Spring Run Farm, Lowell, Indiana

Elaine and Bob Jensen are the owners of a beautiful century-old farm and is the proprietor of one of the finest quality folk art and antique shops in the state.

PEACH POUND CAKE

    1 cup butter, softened (no substitutes)
    2 cups sugar
    6 eggs
    1 teaspoon almond extract
    1 teaspoon vanilla extract
    3 cups all-purpose flour
    ¼ teaspoon baking soda
    ¼ teaspoon salt
    ½ cup sour cream
    2 cups diced fresh or frozen peaches
 Confectioners' sugar

Preheat oven to 350 degrees. In a large mixing bowl, cream butter and sugar until light and fluffy. Add eggs, one at a time, beating well after each addition. Beat in extracts. In a separate bowl, combine the flour, baking soda and salt. Add to the batter alternately with sour cream. Fold in the peaches. Pour into greased and floured 10-inch fluted tube pan. Bake at 350 degrees for 60–70 minutes or until a tooth pick inserted near center comes out clean. Cool for 15 minutes before removing from pan to a wire rack to cool completely. Dust with confectioners' sugar if desired. Serves 12–16.

Marilyn Nemethy and Mary Wendzel, Glad Peach Bake Fest Winners, Coloma, Michigan

LOW-FAT GEORGIA PEACH POUND CAKE

1½ cups sugar, divided
⅓ cup vegetable oil
½ cup plain low fat yogurt
3 eggs
2 egg whites
1 teaspoon vanilla extract
3 cups flour, divided
1½ teaspoons baking powder
½ teaspoon salt
2 cups chopped, fresh Georgia peaches

Spray a 10-inch tube pan with cooking spray. Sprinkle with 1 teaspoon sugar. Combine oil and yogurt, gradually add remaining sugar, beating well. Add whole eggs and whites, one at a time, beating well after each addition. Add vanilla and mix well. Combine 2¾ cups of the flour, baking powder and salt. Gradually add to yogurt mixture; beat until well-blended. Dredge peaches with remaining ¼ cup flour. Fold peaches into batter. Pour batter into prepared pan. Bake at 350 degrees for 1 hour 10 minutes. Remove from pan and cool completely. Yield: 16 servings.

Courtesy of Dickey Farms, Musella, Georgia, "The Sweetest Peaches in the South"

GEORGIA PEACH CRUMBLE CAKE

½ cup unsalted butter, softened
½ cup firmly packed light brown sugar
½ cup plus 3 tablespoons granulated sugar
1 cup sifted all-purpose flour
1 teaspoon baking powder
2 large eggs
10 large Georgia peaches, skinned and cut in half
1 tablespoon fresh lemon juice
½ teaspoon ground cinnamon
Vanilla-flavored whipped cream or ice cream

Preheat oven to 350 degrees. Lightly butter 8-inch square baking dish. Set aside. Cream butter, brown sugar and ½ cup granulated sugar until light and fluffy, about 3 minutes. Sift together the flour and baking powder and beat into the butter mixture. Beat in eggs. Scrape the mixture into the prepared baking dish and place the peach halves on top of the batter, flat side down. Sprinkle with the lemon juice; more if you like. Mix remaining sugar with cinnamon and sprinkle over peaches. You may also increase this amount if you like. Bake for 1 hour, or until golden in color. Serve with flavored whipped cream or ice cream. Yield: 6 to 8 servings.

Courtesy of Dickey Farms, Musella, Georgia, "The Sweetest Peaches in the South"

DUMP CAKE

2 sticks margarine
1 (15¼-ounce) can crushed pineapple, drained
2 cans Comstock cherry pie filling*
1 box yellow cake mix
1–1½ cups chopped pecans
A little cinnamon and sugar mixed together

Preheat oven to 350 degrees. Melt ½ stick of margarine in a 13 x 9-inch cake pan. Drain most of the juice from the pineapple. Dump the pineapple into the cake pan and spread evenly. Dump 2 cans of pie filling on top of pineapple and spread evenly. Then dump the cake mix on top of the pie filling and spread evenly. Then take the other 1½ sticks of margarine and slice thinly all over the cake mix. Sprinkle the chopped pecans all over the top and sprinkle with cinnamon and sugar. Bake at 350 degrees for 1 hour. Enjoy!
*Can use peach or apple pie filling

Thanks to one of my favorite students, Linda Teale

GINGER PEACH UPSIDE DOWN CAKE

1 Betty Crocker gingerbread cake mix
1 can peach pie filling

Preheat oven to 350 degrees. Prepare gingerbread cake batter using directions on box. Line a 9-inch square baking pan with pie filling. Add gingerbread cake batter. Bake in a 350 degree oven for 30 minutes. Remove from oven, invert onto serving plate. Serve warm or cool. Top with whipped cream or frozen whipped topping dollops if desired.

Ashley Hert, Glad Peach Bake Fest Winner, Coloma, Michigan

PEACH UPSIDE DOWN CAKE

½ cup vegetable oil
1 cup packed brown sugar
1 can peach slices
1 jar maraschino cherries, halved
2 eggs
1 box white cake mix
Whipped cream

Preheat oven to 350 degrees. Pour oil into a 13 x 9 x 2-inch baking pan. Sprinkle brown sugar evenly over oil. Drain peaches, reserving peach syrup. Arrange peaches and cherry halves in the sugar mixture. Add enough water to peach juice to make 1⅓ cups liquid. Mix together peach liquid, eggs, and cake mix. Pour batter over the fruit. Bake for 50 to 55 minutes or until cake pulls away from sides of the pan. Let stand 5 minutes, then turn upside down onto serving plate. Serve warm, topped with whipped cream.

Anna Dorris, Glad Peach Bake Fest Winner, Coloma, Michigan

GEORGIA PEACH UPSIDE DOWN CAKE #1

2 pounds Georgia peaches
½ cup light brown sugar
13 tablespoons butter, divided
2¼ cups flour
1½ teaspoons baking soda
¼ teaspoon salt
½ teaspoon ground ginger
½ teaspoon cinnamon
¼ teaspoon ground nutmeg
1 cup granulated sugar
1 egg
1 teaspoon vanilla extract
1½ cups sour cream

Preheat oven to 350 degrees. Peel and halve peaches. Cook brown sugar in 5 tablespoons butter in 10-inch ovenproof frying pan until dissolved. Turn off the heat, arrange peach halves, cut sides up, in pan. Combine flour, baking soda, salt and spices. Beat 8 tablespoons butter with granulated sugar. Beat in egg and vanilla. Stir in flour mixture by thirds, alternating with sour cream. Spread over peaches and bake until toothpick inserted in center comes out clean, 50–55 minutes.

Courtesy of Dickey Farms, Musella, Georgia, "The Sweetest Peaches in the South"

GEORGIA PEACH UPSIDE DOWN CAKE #2

CARAMEL

- 6 tablespoons butter plus additional for pan
- 1 cup sugar
- 4 to 6 fresh Georgia peaches, halved and pitted

Butter a 10-inch cake pan, line the bottom with parchment paper, and butter the paper. Place 2 tablespoons water and sugar in a saucepan, and stir together. Cook over high heat, swirling the pan (do not stir), until the mixture turns a golden caramel color. Immediately remove the pan from the heat, and whisk in the butter (be careful, the mixture will foam). Pour the caramel into the bottom of the prepared cake pan. Cover with peach halves, cut-side-down.

CAKE

- 1 cup granulated sugar
- ½ cup melted butter
- 2 eggs
- 1½ cups all-purpose flour
- 2 teaspoons baking powder
- 1 teaspoon salt
- ½ cup buttermilk
- 2 teaspoons vanilla extract

Preheat oven to 350 degrees. Fit a mixer with a whisk attachment. Beat sugar and melted butter together until combined. Add eggs. Whisk until the mixture is light and fluffy. In a separate bowl, sift together flour, baking powder, and salt. In a small bowl, stir the buttermilk and vanilla extract together. With mixer set on low speed, add the dry ingredients by thirds, alternating with the liquid ingredients, to the butter mixture. When all is fully blended, pour the batter into the pan over the peaches and bake, rotating pan front-to-back after the first 15 minutes, for about 50 minutes or until the cake is golden brown and springy to the touch. Allow to sit for about 10 minutes before inverting onto a platter.

Courtesy of Dickey Farms, Musella, Georgia, "The Sweetest Peaches in the South"

PEACHES AND CREME CHEESECAKE CUPCAKES

PEACH MANGO TOPPING

    2 cups peeled, chopped fresh ripe peaches
    ½ cup mango juice
    ⅓ cup sugar
    2½ tablespoons cornstarch

Combine 1 cup peaches, mango juice, sugar and cornstarch in a medium saucepan. Cook and stir over medium heat until mixture bubbles and thickens. Cool for 10 minutes, then add the remaining 1 cup peaches. Set aside.

CHEESECAKE

    3 (8-ounce) packages cream cheese, softened
    5 eggs
    1 teaspoon vanilla extract
    1 teaspoon almond extract
    1 cup sugar

Preheat oven to 300 degrees. Use an electric mixer to combine all cheesecake ingredients, beat on medium speed until smooth. Place paper baking cups into muffin tins and fill cups two-thirds full with cheesecake batter. Bake for 40 minutes.

SOUR CREAM FILLING

    1 cup sour cream
    3 tablespoons sugar
    1 teaspoon vanilla extract

Mix sour cream filling ingredients in a small mixing bowl using a spoon. When the cupcakes sink in the middle, place a scant tablespoon of sour cream mixture in the middle of each one. Place back into the oven for 5 more minutes. Remove from oven and cool. When cool, spoon about 1½ to 2 tablespoons of Peach Mango Topping over the top of the sour cream filling on each cupcake and refrigerate.

Courtesy of South Carolina Peach Council

Cookies & Bars

PEACH MOLASSES COOKIES

½ cup sugar
1 egg
1½ teaspoons baking soda
½ cup shortening
½ cup molasses
1 cup mashed peaches
½ cup sour milk
½ teaspoon cinnamon
2½ cups flour
1 teaspoon ginger
½ teaspoon salt

Preheat oven to 350 degrees. Cream sugar, egg, baking soda, shortening, molasses, and peaches. Add milk, cinnamon, flour, ginger and salt to creamed mixture. Batter will be moist and stiff. Drop onto a cookie sheet. Bake at 350 degrees for 10–12 minutes. Frost with your favorite cream cheese (optional). Yield 3 dozen.

Jacquelyn Hert, Glad Peach Bake Fest Winner, Coloma, Michigan

BAKED FRESH PEACH MACAROONS

6 medium fresh peaches
1 egg white, stiffly beaten
¼ cup white corn syrup
½ cup firmly packed brown sugar, sifted
2 cups coarse dry bread crumbs

Preheat oven to 350 degrees. Dip peaches in hot water to remove skin. Slowly combine beaten egg white and corn syrup, beating until blended. Add sifted brown sugar and bread crumbs. Cover peach with macaroon mixture. Place on a greased baking sheet and bake in a preheated 350 degree oven for 25 minutes.

PEACH FUZZ COOKIES

1 cup coconut, finely shredded, soaked in
   fresh peach juice, dried and lightly toasted
2 fresh peaches
¾ pound butter
1 cup sugar
2 egg yolks
1 teaspoon vanilla extract
3 cups flour
⅛ teaspoon salt
Peach preserves as needed

Preheat oven to 325 degrees. Cut shredded coconut even finer by placing in deep bowl and cutting with scissors. Soak in juice from 2 peaches. Dry on paper towels, place on cookie sheet. Before toasting, remove paper towel and toast quickly and lightly in oven. Set aside. Coconut can be prepared the night before. Cream butter and sugar, add egg yolks and vanilla. Beat well. Sift flour and salt. Add to creamed mixture. Beat well. Make small balls, roll lightly in coconut. Press with thumb. Fill thumbprint with peach preserves. Bake at 325 degrees for 10 minutes or until light golden brown.

Susan Zeilenga, Glad Peach Bake Fest Winner,
Coloma, Michigan

PEACHY OATMEAL COOKIES

2 cups flour
1½ cups sugar
2 teaspoons baking powder
½ teaspoon salt
½ teaspoon nutmeg
¾ cup butter or margarine
1 egg
¾ cup pureed canned peach halves (drain
   and puree)
2 to 2½ cups oats

Preheat oven to 375 degrees. Sift flour, sugar, baking powder, salt and nutmeg into medium mixing bowl. Add butter, egg and pureed peaches. Beat until smooth. Blend in oats. Dough will be thick. Drop 3 inches apart onto a lightly greased cookie sheet. Bake in preheated oven for 12 to 15 minutes.

Sharon Ball, Glad Peach Bake Fest Winner,
Coloma, Michigan

PEACH BUTTER BALLS

1 cup butter
½ cup confectioners' sugar
½ teaspoon salt
½ cup peach preserves
1 tablespoon vanilla extract
2½ cups flour, sifted

Preheat oven to 350 degrees. In a large mixing bowl, cream butter. Add sugar, salt, and preserves, cream together thoroughly. Add vanilla extract. Gradually blend in flour, mixing thoroughly after each addition. Shape into balls, using a tablespoon of dough for each. Place on un-greased cookie sheet. Bake at 350 degrees for 15–20 minutes. Roll cookies in additional confectioners' sugar before serving.

Pauline Palgen, Glad Peach Bake Fest Winner, Coloma, Michigan

PEACH ALMOND BARS

1 package yellow cake mix with pudding
1 stick butter (8 tablespoons), melted
½ cup finely chopped almonds
1⅓ cups peach preserves (12-ounce jar)
1 (8-ounce) package cream cheese, room temperature
¼ cup sugar
2 tablespoons all purpose flour
½ teaspoon pure almond extract
1 large egg

Preheat oven to 350 degrees. Place cake mix, melted butter and almonds in large mixing bowl. Blend with electric mixer on low for 1½ minutes, mixture should be crumbly. Reserve 1 cup for topping. Transfer remaining crust mixture into a 13 x 9-inch pan. Using fingertips, press evenly over pan. Spread preserves over the crust. Set aside. Place cream cheese in same mixing bowl. Blend with mixer on low for 30 seconds until creamy. Stop mixing and add sugar, flour, almond extract, and egg. Beat on low speed until combined, about 1 to 2 minutes. Spread filling over preserves so that it covers entire surface. Scatter reserved crust mixture over the filling. Bake at 350 degrees for 33–35 minutes. After baking, cool for 30 minutes before cutting into bars. Yield: 24 bars.

Janet Snyder, Glad Peach Bake Fest Winner, Coloma, Michigan

Raise Your Own Luscious Peaches

Red Bird Cling
Very Best Early Peach
Introduced by Stark Bro's

EUREKA
Early White Freestone

PEACH BARS

- 1½ cups flour
- 1½ cups oatmeal
- 1 cup light brown sugar
- 1 teaspoon baking powder
- ¾ cup butter
- 12 ounces peach jam, room temperature

Preheat oven to 350 degrees. Mix dry ingredients with butter, until it is like coarse meal. Pat two-thirds of this mixture into well greased 13 x 9-inch pan. Cover with peach jam at room temperature. Cover with remaining crumbs. Bake for 40 minutes at 350 degrees. Cut into bars while warm. This can be made 3—4 days ahead of time.

Barbara Fay, Glad Peach Bake Fest Winner, Coloma, Michigan

PEACHES 'N CREAM BARS

30 graham cracker squares (15 rectangles)
½ cup sliced almonds
1 cup sugar
6 tablespoons unsalted butter, melted
12 ounces cream cheese, room temperature
2 eggs
1 teaspoon vanilla extract

TOPPING

2 tablespoons cold butter, cut into pieces
¼ cup packed light brown sugar
½ cup sliced almonds
2 tablespoons flour
1 (13-ounce) jar peach preserves

Preheat oven to 350 degrees. Coat a 13 x 9 x 2-inch baking pan with non-stick cooking spray. Combine crackers, almonds and ½ cup sugar in blender. Process until well blended. Pour in melted butter. Process until crumbs hold together. Press into bottom of pan. Bake at 350 degrees for 10 minutes or until light colored.

Meanwhile, beat together cream cheese and ½ cup sugar in a large bowl with electric mixer until smooth. Beat in eggs one at a time, then beat in vanilla. Remove crust from oven. Pour in cream cheese mixture, spread evenly in pan. Return to oven and bake 15 minutes or until slightly puffed. Prepare topping: crumble together cold butter, brown sugar, sliced almonds and flour in bowl. Remove pan from oven. Stir peach preserves to break up clumps. Gently spread peach preserves on top of bars. Sprinkle with topping. Bake another 15 minutes or until hot and bubbly. Cool completely in pan or wire rack for firmer bars, chill in refrigerator. Cut into bars and serve. Yield: About 2 dozen.

Marianne Page, Glad Peach Bake Fest Winner, Coloma, Michigan

SOUR CREAM PEACH BARS

BASE AND TOPPING

- 1 cup packed brown sugar
- 1 cup butter, softened
- 1½ cups flour
- 1 teaspoon baking soda
- 2 cups quick cooking rolled oats

FILLING

- ¾ cup sugar
- 1 teaspoon almond extract
- 1 egg
- ¼ cup flour
- 1 cup sour cream
- 3½ cups chopped peaches, about 6 fresh peaches

Preheat oven to 350 degrees. In large bowl, combine brown sugar and butter, blend well. Lightly spoon flour into measuring cup, level off. Add 1½ cups flour, baking soda and rolled oats. Mix until crumbs form. Press half of crumb mixture into bottom of ungreased 15 x 19 x 1-inch baking pan. Reserve remaining topping. Bake at 350 degrees for 10 minutes. In a large bowl, combine all filling ingredients except peaches, mix well. Add peaches. Pour mixture over partially baked crust. Crumble and sprinkle remaining half of crumb mixture over filling. Bake at 350 degrees for 25–35 minutes or until center is set. Completely cool, then cut bars. Store in refrigerator. Makes 60 bars.

Lisa Parry, Jacquelyn Hert and Cecelia Drake, Glad Peach Bake Fest Winners, Coloma, Michigan

PEACH AND OATS BARS

2 cups flour

1 teaspoon salt

1½ teaspoons baking powder

2 cups quick oats

1½ cups packed brown sugar

1½ cups butter

2 cups peach preserves

Preheat oven to 350 degrees. Mix together flour, salt, and baking powder. Mix in oats and sugar. Cut in butter until crumbly, pat half of the crumbs into a 10 x 14-inch pan. Spread with preserves, top with remaining crumbs. Bake in moderate 375 degree oven for 35 minutes. Cool. Yield: 2½ dozen.

Debra Pena, Glad Peach Bake Fest Winner, Coloma, Michigan

PEACHY CHEESECAKE BARS

CRUST

2 cups flour

¼ cup sugar

½ teaspoon salt

¾ cup butter

⅓ cup corn syrup

FILLING

2 (8-ounce) packages cream cheese, softened

3 eggs

1 cup corn syrup

2 teaspoons vanilla extract

¾ cup peaches (sliced and cooked down)

Preheat oven to 375 degrees. Grease a 13 x 9-inch pan. Set aside. Mix flour, sugar, and salt in medium bowl. Cut in butter until mixture is fine and crumbly. Stir in ⅓ cup corn syrup until a soft dough forms. Press into bottom of prepared baking pan.

In a small bowl, beat cream cheese and eggs with an electric mixer and continue to mix until smooth and creamy. Mix in 1 cup corn syrup and vanilla until well blended. Spread evenly over crust. Bake for 35 to 40 minutes until edges are light brown. Remove from oven and spread ¾ cup peaches over the hot filling. Chill for 3 hours before cutting into small squares.

Clayton Stakley, Glad Peach Bake Fest Winner, Coloma, Michigan

PEACH ROPE SLICES

2   cups flour
½   teaspoon baking powder
½   teaspoon salt
⅔   cup sugar
¾   cup butter, softened
1   egg, beaten
2   teaspoons vanilla extract
½   cup peach pie filling

Preheat oven to 350 degrees. In a mixing bowl, combine flour, baking powder, salt, and sugar. Blend in butter, egg, and vanilla to form dough. Place on lightly floured surface and divide dough into 4 pieces. Shape each piece in a 13-inch rope, ¾-inch thick. Place on ungreased 12 x 14-inch baking sheet. Use the handle of a butter knife to make a ¼-inch deep depression down the center of each rope. Fill depression with peach filling. Bake in a 350 degree oven for 20 minutes or until golden brown. While still warm, cut diagonally into bars and sprinkle with confectioners' sugar.

Marge Baes, Glad Peach Bake Fest Winner, Coloma, Michigan

PEACH SQUARES

A dollop of whipped cream with a small fresh peach leaf adds a special touch.

2½   cups canned peach slices, drained
¾   cup sugar
¼   cup water
1   tablespoon peach brandy (optional)
2   cups sifted all-purpose flour
1   teaspoon salt
½   teaspoon baking soda
¾   cup butter
1   cup sugar
1½   cups flaked coconut
½   cup chopped pecans

Preheat oven to 400 degrees. Combine canned peaches, ¾ cup sugar, water, and brandy, if desired; cook about 5 minutes, stirring occasionally, until slightly thickened. Cool and set aside. Sift flour, salt, and baking soda together. Set aside. In a separate bowl, cream butter, gradually adding 1 cup sugar; beating well. Blend in dry ingredients. Stir in coconut and pecans. Press three cups of this crumbly mixture in bottom and half way up sides of greased 13 x 9 x 2-inch baking pan. Bake in a preheated 400 degree oven for 10 minutes. Spread peach mixture over crust and sprinkle rest of crumbs on top. Bake 20 to 25 minutes. Cool. Cut into squares.

PEACH SQUARES

6 medium ripe peaches, peeled and sliced
½ tablespoon lemon juice
1 cup sugar
½ cup butter, melted
1 cup flour
1 teaspoon baking soda
¼ teaspoon salt

Preheat oven to 350 degrees. Place sliced peaches in bottom of a 9-inch square pan. Sprinkle lemon juice over peaches. In a separate bowl, combine sugar, melted butter, flour, baking soda and salt. Mix until crumbly. Sprinkle over peaches and bake in a pre-heated 350 degree oven for 30 minutes. Serves 8.

ELAINE'S NUTTY PEACH CRISP

1 (29-ounce) can sliced peaches with syrup
1 box Betty Crocker Butter Pecan Cake Mix
½ cup butter, melted
1 cup flaked coconut
1 cup chopped pecans

Preheat oven to 325 degrees. Layer ingredients in order listed in ungreased 13 x 9-inch pan. Bake for 55-60 minutes. Let stand at least 15 minutes before serving. Serve warm or cool. May be served with whipped cream or ice cream. Serves 12–15.

Thanks to Elaine Jensen, Spring Run Farm, Lowell, Indiana

Pies

PEACHES AND CREAM PIE

2 tablespoons flour
2 tablespoons quick cooking tapioca
¼ teaspoon salt
½ cup sugar
1 (9-inch) pie shell
1 cup sour cream
1 cup packed brown sugar
8 good sized peaches

Preheat oven to 450 degrees. Combine flour, tapioca, salt and ½ cup sugar. Spread on bottom and sides of unbaked pie shell. Mix together the sour cream and brown sugar. Set aside. Peel peaches and halve them. Dip each peach in the sugar and cream mixture. Arrange peaches cut side down in pastry shell. Pour remaining sugar and cream mixture over peaches. Sprinkle lightly with nutmeg or cinnamon if you like.

Bake in 450 degree oven for 15 minutes. Reduce heat to 350 degrees and bake additional 30-45 minutes. Can bake longer if peaches are not tender.

Thanks to Elaine Jensen, Spring Run Farm, Lowell, Indiana

BLUSHING PEACH PIE

1 (9-inch) pastry pie crust with lid
2 (29-ounce) cans sliced peaches, drained
½ cup sugar
¼ cup all purpose flour
¼ cup red cinnamon candies
2 tablespoons margarine or butter

Preheat oven to 425 degrees. Prepare pastry. Mix peaches, sugar, flour, and candies. Pour mixture into pie crust. Dot with margarine. Cover with top crust that has slits cut in it. Seal and flute. Cover edge of crust with a 2 to 3-inch strip of aluminum foil to prevent excess browning. Remove foil during last 15 minutes of baking. Bake until crust is golden brown and juice begins to bubble through slits in crust (about 40–50 minutes).

Barbary Fay, Glad Peach Bake Fest Winner, Coloma, Michigan

REFRIGERATOR PEACHES AND CREAM PIE

1½ cups sugar, divided
1 (8-ounce) package cream cheese
1 (8-ounce) tub Cool Whip®
2 graham cracker crust pie shells
3 tablespoons cornstarch
1 small box of peach or apricot Jello®
6 fresh peaches, peeled and sliced

Filling: Cream together ½ cup of the sugar and cream cheese. Add Cool Whip® and mix well. Pour mixture into pie shells and refrigerate until ready for glaze.

Peach Glaze Filling: Cook one cup of the sugar and cornstarch until thick, add Jello®, mix well and let cool. Add peaches to Jello® mixture. Spoon over filling and refrigerate to set.

Joann Frazier, Glad Peach Bake Fest Winner, Coloma, Michigan

PEACH AND CREAM CHEESE PIE

¾ cup all-purpose flour
½ teaspoon salt
1 teaspoon baking powder
1 egg, slightly beaten
3 tablespoons margarine, melted
½ cup milk
1 (3.75-ounce) box instant vanilla pudding
1 (16-ounce) can sliced peaches, drained reserving 3 tablespoons syrup
1 (8-ounce) package cream cheese, softened
½ cup plus 1 tablespoon sugar, divided
½ teaspoon cinnamon

Preheat oven to 350 degrees. In a large bowl, combine flour, salt, baking powder, egg, margarine, milk and pudding mix. Mix well. Spread on bottom and sides of a buttered 9-inch pie plate. Place peaches over top of mix, lining the bottom of the pan. Beat cream cheese, ½ cup sugar and reserved syrup for 2 minutes with an electric mixer. Spread mixture over peaches. Combine 1 tablespoon sugar and cinnamon and sprinkle over top. Bake in preheated oven for 25 minutes. Serves 6.

Thanks to Bettye J. Knott, Waxahachie, Texas

RANGER PEACH CREAM CHEESE PIE

COOKIE CRUST

- ½ cup butter
- ½ cup packed brown sugar
- ½ cup sugar
- 1 egg, well beaten
- ½ teaspoon vanilla extract
- 1 cup flour
- ½ teaspoon baking soda
- ¼ teaspoon baking powder
- ¼ teaspoon salt
- 1 cup oatmeal
- 1 cup corn flakes
- ½ cup coconut
- ¼ cup butter, melted

CREAM CHEESE FILLING

- 2 (8-ounce) packages cream cheese, softened
- 1½ cups powdered sugar
- 1 cup whipping cream
- 2 teaspoons vanilla extract
- ½ teaspoon cinnamon
- ¼ teaspoon nutmeg
- ¼ teaspoon ginger

FRUIT TOPPING

- 4 large peaches, peeled, pitted and sliced
- 1 tablespoon lemon juice
- ½ pint blueberries
- ¼ cup peach jam, melted

To prepare cookie crust: Preheat oven to 350 degrees. Cream butter, sugars, egg, and vanilla. Stir in flour, baking soda and powder, salt, oatmeal, corn flakes and coconut. Drop by rounded tablespoons onto cookie sheet. Bake for 10 minutes. When completely cooled, crumble and mix in medium bowl with ¼ cup melted butter. Pat mixture into bottom and sides of 10-inch glass pie dish, bake until golden, about 8 minutes, in preheated 375 degree oven. Let cool completely.

To prepare filling: Beat cream cheese until smooth, add sugar, whipping cream and vanilla. Divide mixture in half and put into separate bowls. Blend cinnamon, nutmeg, and ginger into one half and spread evenly into crust, then spread plain filling evenly over top. Refrigerate until firm, about 2 hours.

To prepare topping: Toss peaches with lemon juice to prevent discoloration.

After filling has set, arrange sliced peaches in rings around edge of pie, circling inward. Arrange blueberries in center and decorate with additional blueberries as desired. Brush warm jam lightly over fruit to glaze. Refrigerate until ready to serve.

Genevieve Geisler, Glad Peach Bake Fest Winner, Coloma, Michigan

BILL ENDERLE

The "Hill Country" of Texas remembers Bill Enderle as the father of the Hill Country Peach Industry. No one knew the area better than he did since he was the Gillespie County Surveyor for 63 years.

Others grew peaches before him in the area but they only grew enough to be consumed by the local market.

By 1925 the Enderles were producing more peaches than they could market to the small local community. As a boy, Bill Enderle had developed a friendship with the Butt family. "Mother" Butt had become a customer for peaches and would drive to the orchard herself. This connection through her son, H.E. Butt, allowed Enderle to ship his peaches to San Antonio and Austin to the H.E.B. food stores chain. At that time he received a dollar a bushel, delivered to the food chain.

With his new found wealth Enderle was able to lease 30 more acres at three dollars an acre and planted 50 trees per acre. Ten years later he bought 145 acres and on half of it planted nearly 5,000 trees.

One of Enderle's famous clients was Lyndon Johnson. He surveyed much of what is the LBJ ranch and LBJ's father would accompany him as he worked.

Vogel peach orchard.

Lyndon Johnson in front of the school he attended in the Texas Hill Country. Photo by Yoichi R. Okamoto, LBJ Library.

FOOL PROOF PEACHES AND CREAM PIE

FOOL PROOF CRUST

    4 cups flour
1⅓ cup shortening (Crisco)
    1 tablespoon sugar
    1 teaspoon salt
    1 teaspoon vinegar
    1 egg
    ½ cup water

FILLING

    1 cup sugar
    ¼ cup flour
    2 tablespoons quick cooking tapioca
Dash of salt
    1 cup whipping cream, divided
    ¼ teaspoon vanilla extract
    4 cups diced or sliced peaches
Additional sugar

Crust: Mix together flour, shortening, sugar and salt. Cut in shortening until it resembles small peas or meal. In a separate bowl, beat remaining crust ingredients. Combine two mixtures until moistened, mold into ball, chill at least 15 minutes before rolling. Line 9-inch pie pan with crust, trim pastry even with edge of plate. Makes 2 (9-inch) double pie crusts.

Filling: Combine sugar, flour, tapioca and salt. Mix well. Set aside 2 tablespoons of the whipping cream. Combine remaining cream and vanilla and add to sugar mixture. Add peaches, toss to coat. Let stand 15 minutes. Pour into crust. Roll out remaining pastry, put over fruit and seal edges. Brush with reserved cream, sprinkle with additional sugar. Cover crust edges loosely with foil for 30 minutes. Bake at 375 degrees for 50–55 minutes or until crust is brown and fruit is bubbly.

Mary Wendzel, Glad Peach Bake Fest Winner, Coloma, Michigan

CRUMB-TOPPED PEACH PIE

1 (9-inch) deep dish pie crust, unbaked
1 cup sugar
⅓ cup cornstarch
⅛ teaspoon salt
1 egg, beaten
½ teaspoon almond extract
6 cups peaches, peeled, sliced

TOPPING

¼ cup sugar
¼ cup packed brown sugar
½ cup flour
¼ cup margarine

Preheat oven to 375 degrees.

Mix sugar, cornstarch and salt in a large bowl. Add egg and almond extract, mix well. Add peach slices to bowl, toss gently to coat with sugar mixture. Arrange peach slices in pie crust.

For topping: combine sugar, brown sugar and flour in a small bowl. Cut in margarine using pastry blended or 2 knives, until crumbly. Sprinkle topping over peaches. Bake until golden brown abo0ut 30 minutes. Serve pie warm or cold.

Mary Harrell, Glad Peach Bake Fest Winner, Coloma, Michigan

DR. STANLEY JOHNSTON

South Haven is known for horticulturist, Dr. Stanley Johnston. His father was a student of Dr. L.H. Bailey Jr. Dr. Johnston's plant research led him to develop the Haven varieties of which the Red Haven peach has become the most well known peach in the world. He was Director of the South Haven Experiment Station. He personally brought Michigan from raising no blueberries to being the nation's largest producer of blueberries. His many accomplishments and contributions to the horticultural industry all over the world were recognized when he was inducted into the American Society or Horticultural Science Hall of Fame.

Many of the farms dotting the landscape of the S.W. Michigan fruitbelt in the late 1800's are now currently being farmed by fourth and fifth generation members of the original families. Some of these families and farms are pictured in this book. These pictures mirror a kaleidoscope of color, tree form, soil texture, light and shade. All of these leave an indelible mark on our souls and make us envy the artists who capture on canvas the fleeting vignettes of each of the peach farms.

BETTYE'S FAVORITE PEACH PIE

1 can pie sliced peaches (can also use apples), well drained
1 cup packed brown sugar
½ cup sugar
1 teaspoon white vinegar
½ teaspoon cinnamon
¼ teaspoon nutmeg
2 tablespoons flour
¼ teaspoon salt
2 (9-10-inch) unbaked pie crusts
2 tablespoons butter

Preheat oven to 425 degrees. Drain fruit. Combine fruit, sugars, vinegar, cinnamon, nutmeg, flour, and salt. Pour into unbaked pie crust. Dot filling with butter. Cover with second pie shell. Crimp edges of crust to seal in juice. Make slits in top crust to vent. Bake in preheated 425 degree oven for 10 minutes. Reduce heat to 350 degrees and continue to bake for 30-40 minutes or until crust is golden brown. You may need to make a tent of foil around the edges of the crust to prevent burning.

Thanks to Bettye J. Knott, Waxahachie, Texas

GRANNY ODELL'S PEACH PIE

CRUST

⅔ cup Crisco
2 cups flour
½ teaspoon salt
⅓ cup water

Blend crisco, 1⅔ cups flour, and salt with a pastry blender until like fine cornmeal. Add remaining ⅓ cup flour and water. Knead well and roll out thin. Use a 9-inch pie plate. Set aside.

FILLING

1 quart fresh or canned ripe peaches
½ cup sugar
2 eggs
1 tablespoon flour
¼ pound margarine, melted
1 teaspoon vanilla extract

Preheat oven to 350 degrees. Drain juice from peaches. Line unbaked pie shell with peaches, sprinkle sugar over peaches. Mix next four ingredients; pour over peaches. Bake in a preheated 350 degree oven for 15 minutes. Turn oven down to 325 degrees and bake until a knife inserted into the center comes out clean.

PEACH DEEP DISH PIE

4 cups sliced Michigan peaches
1 tablespoon lemon juice
1 cup flour
1 cup sugar
½ cup butter, melted

Preheat oven to 400 degrees. Arrange peaches on bottom of 9-inch deep dish pie plate; drizzle with lemon juice. Combine flour, sugar and melted butter, blending with a pastry blender to coarse crumbs. Sprinkle mixture over peaches. Bake in preheated oven for about 40 minutes.

PEACH CUSTARD PIE

Very ripe peaches

1 egg

1 tablespoon flour

1½ cupfuls milk

½ cupful sugar

Cover a pie tin with an unbaked crust. Take fresh peaches, halve, pare and stone them and place a layer, hollow side up in the pie crust. Prepare a custard with the egg, flour, milk, and sugar. Pour this over the peaches and bake. If preferred, the yolks of two eggs may be used in place of one whole egg, and a meringue made of the whites for the top.

From: Vegetarian Cook Book – Israelite House of David, as reorganized by Mary Purnell, 1934

CREAM PEACH PIE

What moistens the lip and what brightens the eye, what brings back the past like a rich peach pie!

Line a deep pie pan with pie crust and fill with sliced peaches. Beat together and pour over the peaches two eggs, ½ cup sugar, 1 tablespoon flour, and 3 tablespoons cream. Bake. If peaches are tart, add more sugar.

Pie Crust
3 cups flour, 1 cup lard, ½ cup cold water, ½ tsp salt. This will make 3 pies.

Mrs. J.N. Parker, Elkhart, Indiana Choice Recipes Compiled by the Ladies Aid of the United Brethren Church, Berrien Springs, Michigan 1924

FRESH PEACH PIE

1 small (6-ounce) can fresh frozen orange juice

1 cup sugar

2 cups water

4 tablespoons cornstarch

1 teaspoon almond flavoring

3 fresh peaches (or can use canned)

1 baked pastry shell (size?)

½ to 1 cup whipping cream flavored to taste with sugar and vanilla

Dilute orange juice with 2 cups water, add sugar and cornstarch. Cook until thickened and bubbling. Add almond flavoring. Remove from heat and cool slightly. Slice fresh peeled peaches into pre-baked pie shell. Cover with filling and let stand for about 1 hour. Cover with whipped cream and serve. Garnish top with sliced peaches if desired. Serves 5.

BAKED PEACH PIE

I triple this recipe to make two pies. We like more filling.

Peeled peaches, halved
1 *(9-inch) unbaked pie shell*
1 *cup sugar*
⅓ *cup margarine*
⅓ *cup flour*
1 *egg, beaten*
¼ *teaspoon vanilla extract*

Preheat oven to 300 degrees. Put peach halves, cut side down into shell. Cream sugar and margarine. Add remaining ingredients and mix well. Spread over peaches. Bake 1 hour at 300 degrees until top is light brown and crusty.

Thanks to Barbara Reisig

UNBAKED PEACH PIE

2 *cups water*
1½ *cups sugar*
½ *teaspoon yellow food color*
4 *tablespoons corn starch*
1 *(3-ounce) package peach Jello®*
Sliced peaches
1 *(9-inch) baked pie shell*

Mix water, sugar, food coloring and cornstarch. Cook until thick and glossy. Add Jello® and let cool. Add peaches and pour into pie shell. Refrigerate. Serve with Cool Whip®.

Thanks to Barbara Reisig

Fruit farm home of J.K. Barden and son, Casco, Michigan. Photo Courtesy Dr. Paul Rood and the State Horticultural Society of Michigan

GROCERY BAG PEACH PIE

1 (9-inch) deep dish unbaked pie crust
2 tablespoons flour
½ teaspoon cinnamon
½ teaspoon nutmeg
¼ cup sugar
3 cups peaches, peeled and sliced
1 brown paper bag

TOPPING

½ cup flour
½ cup packed brown sugar
½ cup butter or margarine

Toss peaches with flour, cinnamon, nutmeg and sugar. Pour into unbaked pie shell. Combine topping ingredients, mix until crumbly. Sprinkle on top of pie. Place pie into brown paper bag, fold and shut tightly. Bake 1½ hours at 350 degrees. Don't open or check until done. Make sure bag doesn't touch top element of oven.

Linda Dasse, Glad Peach Bake Fest Winner, Coloma, Michigan

NONE BUT THE BEST WILL BEAR THIS LABEL
SPAR·CO
SOUTH CAROLINA PEACHES

ORANGE PEACH MERINGUE PIE

1 (16-ounce) can sliced peaches, chopped
1 cup orange juice
½ cup sugar
3 tablespoons cornstarch
¼ cup water
Dash of salt
2 egg yolks, beaten
⅛ teaspoon almond extract
1 teaspoon vanilla extract
3 tablespoons butter
1 (9-inch) pie shell, baked and cooled

MERINGUE

2 egg whites
6 tablespoons sugar
1 teaspoon baking powder
Pinch of salt

Preheat oven to 350 degrees. Drain juice from peaches. In a double boiler, combine peaches and orange juice. Make a paste of sugar, cornstarch, salt, egg yolks and water. Add to juice mixture. Cook over low to medium heat, stirring constantly until thick. Remove from heat and add flavors and butter, stirring until smooth. Add drained peaches. Mix gently and let cool. Pour into pie shell. Beat egg whites until stiff. Add sugar, salt and baking powder. Mix until stiff peaks form. Spread meringue over pie and brown in a 350 degree oven for about 15 minutes.

Grace Scoma, Glad Peach Bake Fest Winner, Coloma, Michigan

FRESH PEACH ALMOND UPSIDE DOWN PIE

Pastry for 2 9-inch pie crusts
- 2 tablespoons butter, softened
- 2/3 cup toasted sliced almonds or pecan halves
- 1/3 cup packed brown sugar
- 5 cups peaches, sliced
- 3/4 cup sugar
- 2 tablespoons tapioca
- 1/4 teaspoon cinnamon
- 1/2 teaspoon nutmeg

Line a 9-inch pan with 12-inch square foil. Let excess foil hang over edge. Spread 2 tablespoons butter on foil, press nuts and brown sugar into butter. Fit bottom pie crust into pie pan over nuts and brown sugar. Mix rest of ingredients. Pour into pastry shell. Cover with top crust, seal, flute and prick with a fork. Brush lightly with milk. Bake at 450 degrees for 10 minutes. Lower heat to 375 degrees and bake 35—40 minutes. Cool thoroughly, turn upside down on serving plate. Remove foil.

Marilyn Nemethy, Glad Peach Bake Fest Winner,
Coloma, Michigan

FRESH BLUEBERRY PEACH PIE

½ *cup sugar*
1½ *tablespoons cornstarch*
½ *teaspoon ground lemon peel*
¼ *teaspoon cinnamon*
Dash salt

Combine all ingredients in a small bowl and set aside.

Bake a frozen 9-inch pie crust or prepare and bake your favorite crust from scratch.

½ *cup (scant) blueberries, divided*
½ *cup (scant) peaches, sliced, divided*
⅔ *cup water*
1 *teaspoon lemon juice*
½ *cup blueberries, reserved*
½ *cup sliced fresh peaches, reserved*
Whipped cream

In a sauce pan, combine ¼ cup blueberries, ¼ cup peaches, and water. Bring mixture to a boil and mash. Add sugar mix slowly to saucepan, stirring continually over medium heat until sauce thickens and bubbles. Add ¼ cup blueberries, ¼ cup peaches, and lemon juice, while gently stirring. Let mixture cool. Add reserved fresh blueberries and peaches. Pour into prepared pie shell. Cool for 2 hours. Top with whipped cream.

Thanks to Barbara A. Farris, Lawton, Michigan

GEORGIA PEACH PRALINE PIE

½ *cup firmly packed brown sugar*
¼ *cup all-purpose flour*
3 *tablespoons cold butter*
½ *cup chopped pecans*
4 *cups fresh ripe sliced Georgia peaches*
2 *tablespoons plus 1 teaspoon all-purpose flour*
⅔ *cup sugar*
1 *teaspoon fresh lemon juice*
1 *(9-inch) unbaked pie shell*

Preheat oven to 425 degrees. Prepare the praline topping by combining the brown sugar and ¼ cup flour and cut in the butter with a pastry blender until mixture has a crumbly texture. Stir in the chopped pecans. Sprinkle one-third of the mixture in the bottom of the unbaked pie shell.

Combine the sliced peaches, 2 tablespoons flour, sugar and lemon juice, and pour into pie shell over praline mixture. Sprinkle remaining praline mixture evenly over peaches. Bake for 45 to 50 minutes, or until syrup boils in heavy bubbles that do not burst. Serve warm, with or without vanilla ice cream.

Courtesy of Dickey Farms, Musella, Georgia, "The Sweetest Peaches in the South"

DREAMY PEACH PIE

1⅔ cups pretzel crumbs

6 tablespoons (¾-stick) unsalted butter at room temperature

¼ cup water

1 envelope unflavored gelatin

1¼ cups peaches, sliced

¼ cup confectioners' sugar

1 (4-ounce) package fat free or light cream cheese, at room temperature

1 cup heavy cream

Knead together pretzel crumbs and butter in plastic food storage bag. Press over bottom and sides of a 9-inch pie plate. Chill in refrigerator. Boil water in a small saucepan. Remove from heat. Sprinkle gelatin over top. Let stand for 5 minutes to soften. Stir to dissolve. Reserve some peaches for garnish, transfer rest to food processor. Process until coarsely chopped. Add sugar and cream cheese, blend, transfer to a large bowl. Beat cream and confectioners' sugar in a medium bowl until soft peaks form. Set aside ⅓ cup whipped cream, fold remainder into peach mixture. Stir in gelatin mixture. Spread mixture in pretzel shell. Dollop reserved whipped cream on top. Garnish with reserved peaches. Chill 1¼ hours. Serves 8.

Marilyn Nemethy, Glad Peach Bake Fest Winner, Coloma, Michigan

ELAINE'S CREAMY PEACH PIE

1 (3-ounce) package peach Jello®

⅔ cup boiling water

1 cup vanilla ice cream, thawed

1 (8-ounce) carton frozen whipped topping

1 cup diced, peeled, fresh peaches

1 (9-inch) deep dish pie shell, baked

Sliced peaches and mint for garnish

In a large bowl, dissolve Jello® in boiling water. Stir in ice cream until melted and add whipped topping. Mix well. Fold in peaches. Pour into pie shell. Chill until firm (about 3 hours). Garnish with peaches and mint, if desired.

Thanks to Elaine Jensen, Spring Run Farm, Lowell, Indiana

Fiorini Ranch

Francis Fiorini immigrated from Italy to Califorina and purchased his 320 acre dry land dairy farm in 1909. With the introduction of irrigation in 1920 the Fiorinis began growing cling peaches and grapes on their ranch. Today nearly 100% if all cling peaches produced are grown in California and are sold processed. Cling peaches are rarely found fresh in the markets.

Peaches contribute $943 million to California's total economy. What started as a simple farm is now known as Fiorini Ranch, owned and entrusted to the Randy Fiorini family, grandson of its founder Francis. If you are unfamiliar with the Turlock, California, you are in for a treat. There is something special about the undiscovered charm of the area.

Randy Fiorini was the youngest person elected chairman of the California Cling Peach Board. He either serves as chairman, president, director or participates as an active member in ten different organizations and charities. The organizations he supports range from the California Cling Peach Board to the California Farm Water Coalition and Hope Unlimited International. Randy was appointed to the Fruits and Vegetables Agricultural Technical Advisory Committee for Trade (ATAC). As a committee member he is called upon to provide information and advice relating to U.S. Agricultural Trade Policies.

Fiorini presently grows 12 to 14 cling peach varieties on 300 acres. His son Jay has a B.A. in Pomology (the science of fruit and nut production) and has joined Fiorini Ranch as a partner.

FARM PEACH PAN PIE

EGG YOLK PASTRY

5 cups flour

4 teaspoons sugar

½ teaspoon salt

½ teaspoon baking powder

1½ cups shortening

2 egg yolks, slightly beaten

¾ cup cold water

FILLING

5 pounds peaches, peeled and thinly sliced

4 teaspoons lemon juice

¾ cup sugar

¾ cup packed brown sugar

1 teaspoon ground cinnamon

½ teaspoon nutmeg

¼ teaspoon salt

Milk

Additional sugar

Preheat oven to 400 degrees.

Egg Yolk Pastry: In a bowl, combine flour, sugar, salt, and baking powder. Cut in shortening until mixture resembles coarse crumbs. Combine egg yolks and cold water, and sprinkle over dry ingredients. Toss with a fork. If needed, add additional water, 1 tablespoon at a time, until mixture can be formed into a ball. Divide dough in half on a lightly floured surface, roll half of dough to fit a 15 x 10 x 1-inch jelly roll pan.

Filling: Sprinkle peaches with lemon juice. Arrange half of peaches over dough. Combine sugars, cinnamon, nutmeg, and salt. Sprinkle half of mixture over peaches. Top with remaining peaches, sprinkle with remaining sugar mixture. Roll remaining pastry to fit pan. Place on top of filling and seal edges. Brush with milk and sprinkle with sugar. Cut vents in top of pastry. Bake at 400 degrees for 50 minutes or until crust is golden brown and filling is bubbly. Makes 18–24 servings.

Nancy Perry, Glad Peach Bake Fest Winner, Coloma, Michigan

PEACH PIE WITH GINGERSNAP STREUSEL

CRUST

- 1¼ cups all-purpose flour
- 2 tablespoons sugar
- ¼ teaspoon salt
- ¼ teaspoon ground ginger
- 4 tablespoons butter, chilled
- 3 tablespoons vegetable shortening
- 4–5 tablespoons ice water

FILLING

- 2 teaspoons cornstarch
- 6 cups peeled, pitted and sliced peaches,
- ¼ cup sugar
- ½ cup packed brown sugar
- 2 teaspoons lemon juice
- ¼ teaspoon each allspice, nutmeg, cinnamon, ginger

TOPPING:

- 6 tablespoons flour
- 6½ cups ginger snap crumbs
- ¼ cup packed brown sugar
- ¼ teaspoon each cinnamon, ginger, nutmeg
- 8 tablespoons unsalted butter, chilled

Crust: Whisk together flour, sugar, salt and ginger. Cut in chunks of butter until mixture is pea sized. Stir in water until dough just clings together. Gather in ball, flatten into disk shape and chill at least one hour. Roll crust out and put into a 9-inch pie pan, gimp edges.

Filling: Mix all ingredients, let sit at least 30 minutes, pour into unbaked pie shell.

Topping: Preheat oven to 400 degrees. Mix dry ingredients in a small bowl. Cut in butter until it reaches small chunk consistency, but not so much that topping forms a sticky dough. Sprinkle on top of filled pie. Bake pie on a baking sheet for 20–25 minutes or when edges are golden and topping has begun to crisp. Reduce temperature to 350 degrees and bake 30–40 minutes more until pie just bubbles and crust is golden but not dark brown.

Genevieve Geisler, Glad Peach Bake Fest Winner, Coloma, Michigan

RIBBON OF PEACH CHEESECAKE

CRUST

- ½ cup chopped pecans
- 1 cup graham cracker crumbs
- ¼ cup butter
- 2 tablespoons sugar

PEACH PUREE

- 1 (21-ounce) can peach filling
- 2 tablespoons cornstarch
- 2 tablespoons brown sugar
- 1 teaspoon almond extract

CHEESE FILLING

- 3 (8-ounce) packages cream cheese (at room temperature)
- ½ cup sour cream (at room temperature)
- 1 can Eagle Brand® sweetened condensed milk
- 1 teaspoon vanilla extract
- 3 eggs, slightly beaten

Preheat oven to 350 degrees. Combine pecans, graham crackers, butter and sugar. Press into a 9-inch spring form pan. Set aside. Puree peach filling until smooth. Combine cornstarch and brown sugar. Stir into pureed peaches. Heat until thick and bubbly. Remove from heat and stir in almond extract. Set aside to cool. Combine cream cheese, sour cream, condensed milk and vanilla in a mixing bowl. Beat at medium speed for 3 to 4 minutes. Add eggs all at once and beat on low speed until mixed. Pour one-third of cream cheese mixture into prepared crust. Top with ⅓ cup of peach puree mixture. Swirl peach mixture into cream cheese mixture, using a knife. Repeat layers twice, ending with peach puree. Reserve remaining puree for topping. Bake at 350 degrees for 1 hour or until center appears set. Let cool on wire rack. When cheesecake is cool, top with remaining puree. Refrigerate until ready to serve.

Marge Baes, Glad Peach Bake Fest Winner, Coloma, Michigan

FRUIT TOPPED GOAT CHEESECAKE

Unsalted butter, for buttering pan

- ¾ pound chevre cheese, at room temperature
- ¾ cup plus 2 tablespoons sugar
- 1 teaspoon lemon zest
- 1½ teaspoons freshly squeezed lemon juice
- 1 teaspoon pure vanilla extract
- 6 large eggs, separated
- 3 tablespoons all-purpose flour
- 3 large Georgia peaches, peeled and cut into ¼-inch slices
- ½ cup blueberries

Confectioners' sugar

Whipped cream or crème fraiche, optional

Preheat oven to 350 degrees. Butter a 9-inch round cake pan, and dust with 1 tablespoon sugar.

In the bowl of an electric mixer fitted with the paddle attachment, combine the cheese with ¾ cup sugar, lemon zest, lemon juice, and vanilla. Beat on medium speed until smooth. Beat in egg yolks, one at a time, incorporating each one completely before adding the next. Reduce to low speed, and add flour.

In another bowl, using the whisk attachment, beat egg whites until stiff. Beat one-third of the egg whites into cheese mixture. Gently fold in remaining egg whites. Pour batter into prepared pan. Bake until deep golden brown and a toothpick inserted in the center comes out clean, 35 to 40 minutes. Cool for 15 minutes on a wire rack. Remove cake from pan, and return to wire rack until completely cooled. In a medium bowl, mix peaches and blueberries with remaining 1 tablespoon sugar. (You may need more sugar, depending on the sweetness of the fruit.) Set aside. When ready to serve, invert the cake onto a serving plate. Dust with confectioner's sugar, and spoon the fruit over the cake, leaving a 1-inch border all the way around. Cut, and serve. Yield: 8 to 10 servings.

Courtesy of Dickey Farms, Musella, Georgia, "The Sweetest Peaches in the South"

PEACH CHEESECAKE

1 (8-ounce) package cream cheese, softened
1 can sweetened condensed milk
1 cup peeled and sliced peaches
½ teaspoon vanilla extract
1 ready to serve graham cracker crust
Whipped topping
Peach slices and leaves for garnish

Mix cream cheese until smooth. Add milk, peaches, and vanilla. Beat until smooth. Pour into crust and refrigerate 2 hours or longer. Before serving, top cake with whipped topping and garnish.

Joseph Maeder, Glad Peach Bake Fest Winner, Coloma, Michigan

PEACHY CHEESECAKE DELIGHT

1 (8-ounce) package cream cheese, softened
¼ to ½ cup honey (depending on your own taste)
1 egg
1 tablespoon lemon juice
½ teaspoon vanilla extract
4 drops peach flavoring
1 ready to serve graham cracker crust
Whipped cream
9 peach slices, peeled, (canned or frozen okay to use)
Pinch of ground nutmeg

Preheat oven to 350 degrees. In a small mixing bowl, beat cream cheese and honey until smooth. Add egg. Beat on low speed until just combined. Stir in lemon juice, vanilla extract, and peach flavoring. Pour into crust. Bake at 350 degrees for 14-18 minutes or until center is almost set. Cool on wire rack for 1 hour. Cover and refrigerate 2 hours or until chilled. Just before serving, top cheesecake with whipped cream and place peach slices along edge of pie. Sprinkle a small amount of nutmeg in center.

Anthony Jackson, Glad Peach Bake Fest Winner, Coloma, Michigan

PEACH CHEESECAKE

1 cup finely chopped fresh peaches
2 cups small curd cottage cheese
1 teaspoon salt
½ cup peach juice
2 tablespoons lemon juice
1 package orange flavored gelatin
1 cup whipping cream
¼ cup sugar
¾ cup crushed graham cracker crumbs
3½ tablespoons melted butter
4 tablespoons finely chopped walnuts

Combine chopped peaches, cottage cheese and salt. Set aside. Heat peach juice to boiling; add lemon juice. Remove from heat and pour over orange gelatin. Stir until dissolved. Cool to room temperature. Beat cheese mixture into cooled gelatin. Whip cream and then fold in sugar. Fold whipped cream into cheese mixture. Spoon into a 6-cup mold. Chill until firm. Turn mixture out of mold onto a serving plate. Combine graham cracker crumbs, butter and walnuts. Sprinkle evenly over top and sides of cheesecake. Serve with sliced peaches. Serves 8.

Memo

Peach Fritters

Pare and remove stone. Slice and dip in a batter made of one cup of flour, ½ cup of milk, two teaspoons sugar, dash of salt, and two eggs. Beat all well together until it becomes a smooth batter. Have ready hot oil as in frying doughnuts, dip the fruit into the batter, drop into the hot oil, and fry about five minutes. Drain and serve with powdered sugar.

From: Vegetarian Cook Book, Eden Springs, Israelite House of David, 1912

PEACH FRITTERS

4 *large ripe peaches*

4 *tablespoons sugar*

4 *tablespoons lemon juice, or 2 tablespoons lemon juice and 2 tablespoons wine*

BATTER FOR FRUIT FRITTERS

1 *cup flour*

2 *tablespoons sugar*

½ *teaspoon salt*

Grated rind 1 lemon

2 *eggs, separated*

½ *cup milk*

Fruit preparation: Remove skins from peaches. Cut each peach into four equal parts. Sprinkle with sugar, lemon juice or lemon juice and wine, and let stand one hour. Dip in fritter batter; fry in deep fat; drain on brown paper. Serve.

Batter preparation: Mix and sift the dry ingredients; add beaten yolks, lemon rind, and mild. Beat, cut, and fold in the beaten whites of eggs and use for any kinds of fruits.

Desserts

DEE HOGE'S PEACH COBBLER

Others call it a sleepy little town, near several nationally known wineries, I call it home. Bill's Tap, known for fine food, attracts an eclectic crowd of locals and the elite of Chicago.

4 cups fresh peeled sliced peaches

1½ cups sugar, divided

½ teaspoon almond extract

6 tablespoons melted butter

¾ cup flour

Pinch salt

2 teaspoons baking powder

¼ teaspoon cinnamon

¾ cup milk

Preheat oven to 350 degrees. Toss peaches, add one cup sugar and extract. Set aside. Pour melted butter into 8 x 8-inch baking dish. In a bowl, mix flour, salt, remaining sugar, baking powder and cinnamon. Stir in milk. Mix well and then pour over butter. Do not stir. Top with peaches. Bake at 350 degrees for 55 minutes.

Courtesy of Chef Dee Hoge, Bill's Tap, Baroda, Michigan

SHINY TOP COBBLER

5 cups unsweetened peaches

1½ tablespoons lemon juice

2 cups flour

3 cups sugar, divided

1 cup milk

½ cup butter, softened and cut into small pieces

2 teaspoons baking powder

2 tablespoons cornstarch

1 teaspoon salt, divided

1½ cups boiling water

Preheat oven to 375 degrees. Spread peaches in a well greased 13 x 9 x 2-inch pan. Sprinkle peaches with lemon juice. Stir flour, 1½ cups of the sugar, milk, butter, baking powder, and ½ teaspoon salt until well blended. (Batter will be thick.) Spoon batter over peaches, spread to edge of baking dish. Mix remaining sugar, cornstarch and salt well and sprinkle over batter. Pour boiling water over batter. Bake in 375 degree oven for 60 minutes or until golden brown and glazed. Serve warm or cool with whipped cream. Serves 12.

Grace Scoma, Glad Peach Bake Fest Winner – 2003, Coloma, Michigan

PEACH COBBLER

2 cups bread flour

4 teaspoons baking powder

½ teaspoon salt

¼ cup solid vegetable shortening

1 egg yolk, slightly beaten

½ cup milk

6 peach halves

12 blanched almonds, cut into pieces

½ cup sugar

¼ teaspoon cinnamon

1 tablespoon butter

Preheat oven to 400 degrees. Sift together the flour, baking powder and salt. Cut in shortening. Set aside. In a small bowl, combine beaten egg yolk and milk and add to flour mixture, forming a soft dough. Roll dough into two squares, about ¼-inch thick. Place one square in a greased square baking dish, arrange peach halves on dough. Add almonds, sugar and cinnamon. Dot mixture with butter and cover with second dough square. Prick with a fork. Bake in preheated oven for about 30 minutes. Cut into squares and serve with whipped cream. Serves 6.

PEACH OR APPLE COBBLER

6 cups peaches

½ cup butter or margarine

1½ cups sugar, reserve ½ cup

1 teaspoon vanilla extract

½ cup milk

1 cup flour

1 teaspoon baking powder

¼ teaspoon salt

½ water

Put a fat layer of fresh peaches into an 8 x 8-inch pan (Double this recipe if you use a 9 x 13-inch pan).

Cream together butter and 1 cup of sugar. Add vanilla, milk, flour, baking powder and salt. Mix well and pour over peaches.

Sprinkle ½ cup sugar over batter, then sprinkle ½ cup water over sugar. Bake 350 degrees for 1 hour.

Thanks to Dorothy Thar

PEACH COBBLER

2 cups sliced peaches
1 cup sugar
1 stick margarine

BATTER

1 cup sugar
¾ cup flour
2 teaspoons baking powder
½ teaspoon salt
¾ cup milk

Preheat oven to 350 degrees.

Mix sliced peaches with sugar. Set aside. Melt margarine in a 9-inch pan in a 350 degree oven.

Beat all batter ingredients until smooth. Pour into pan. Do not stir after pouring over butter.

Top with peaches. Do not stir. Bake at 350 degrees for 45–55 minutes or until browned.

Thanks to Carole Shafer

ESSIE'S COBBLER

¼ cup butter, softened
½ cup sugar
1 cup Gold Medal Flour, sifted
¼ teaspoon salt
2 teaspoons baking powder
½ cup milk

Drained sliced peaches, or cherries, boysenberries, blueberries from a 20-ounce can

¼ to ½ cup sugar (judged by sweetness of fruit)
1 cup fruit juice

Preheat oven to 350 degrees. Cream together butter and ½ cup sugar until fluffy. In a separate bowl, sift together flour, salt and baking powder. Add dry ingredients to creamed mixture, alternating with milk. Beat until smooth. Pour into 10 x 5 x 3-inch loaf pan or use a 2-quart casserole. Spoon fruit over batter; sprinkle with sugar to taste. Pour fruit juice over top. Bake 45 to 50 minutes in preheated 350 degree oven.

During baking the fruit and juice fall to the bottom and a cake-like layer forms on top. Serve warm with whipped cream or good quality vanilla ice cream.

Thanks to Delores Zunk, Hooker, Oklahoma

JOE WATSON

Meeting Joe Watson was like confronting a puzzle, with many pieces. Joe, his brother Jerry and Joe's son Jeph (Joseph H. III) are the current owners of Jerrold A Watson and Sons in Monetta, South Carolina. The logo of the farm is "Watsonia", a name their grandmother created when they were shipping peaches by rail. They had to name their sidetrack at the old packing house and the name Watson was already taken, so she created this new name for their product. The name Watsonia has remained the name of the farm and continues to be the name under which they pack their peaches.

These three men, along with their families, share the love of their farm, just as their forefathers did. With over 1,000 acres of trees reaching to the sky and roots securely grounded in the earth, "The Ridge" is a true unity of heaven and earth.

In 1928 Joe H. Watson gathered four leading farmers from the area together and asked them each to plant 60 acres of peaches. This was the start of the commercial peach industry on "The Ridge" section of South Carolina. The Ridge section is located in the middle of the state is approximately 25 miles long and between 1 and 3 miles wide and stands 600 feet above sea level. This special area is protected during spring frost, because it remains up to 10 degrees warmer at the top than on the sloping sides. The soils are "well drained", with loamy to sandy loam top soil with a clay or loam subsoil between 12 and 24 inches underneath. This is ideal for growing strong, healthy peach trees.

Watsonia Peaches can be found in fine grocery stores from Cleveland to Houston. Picking starts with the Summer Prince Variety in May and ends in September with Autumn Prince. The labors of love continue year round with other fruits and vegetable crops. The facility has Primus Food Safety Certification, an organic certification from Clemson University Department of Plant Industry and the USDA National Organic Program. The Watsons are forerunners in the industry, employing cutting edge agricultural practices.

PEACH COBBLER

This cobbler is a double decker dessert!

8 cups sliced Georgia peaches
2 cups sugar
3 tablespoons all-purpose flour
½ teaspoon nutmeg
1 teaspoon vanilla extract
⅓ cup butter or margarine
Pastry for double crust pie
Vanilla ice cream

Combine peaches, sugar, flour, and nutmeg in a Dutch oven; set aside to allow syrup to form (about 15 minutes) Bring peach mixture to a boil; reduce heat to low, and simmer about 10 minutes or until peaches are tender. Remove from heat and stir in vanilla and butter. Set aside.

Roll half of pastry to a ⅛-inch thickness; cut into a circle to fit a 2-quart baking dish. Spoon half of the peach mixture into lightly buttered baking dish; top with pastry. Bake at 375 degrees for 12 minutes or until lightly brown. Spoon remaining peach mixture over baked pastry.

Roll remaining pastry to ⅛-inch thickness and cut into 1-inch strips; arrange in a lattice design over peaches. Bake an additional 15–20 minutes until browned. Allow to cool slightly before serving. Serve with vanilla ice cream. Serves 8.

Courtesy of Georgia Department of Agriculture

GEORGIA PEACH COBBLER WITH CINNAMON-SWIRL BISCUITS

BISCUT LAYER

- 1 cup all-purpose flour
- 1 tablespoon brown sugar
- 1½ teaspoons baking powder
- ⅛ teaspoon baking soda
- ¼ teaspoon salt
- ¼ cup butter
- ⅓ cup milk
- ½ cup finely chopped walnuts
- 3 tablespoons brown sugar
- ¼ teaspoon ground cinnamon
- 1 tablespoon butter, melted

FILLING

- ⅔ cup packed brown sugar
- 4 teaspoons cornstarch
- ½ teaspoon finely shredded lemon peel
- 6 cups sliced, peeled Georgia peaches
- Sour Cream Topping (recipe below) or ice cream

SOUR CREAM TOPPING

- ½ cup dairy sour cream,
- 1 tablespoon brown sugar
- ⅛ teaspoon ground cinnamon

Preheat oven to 400 degrees.

Biscuit layer: In a medium mixing bowl stir together flour, the brown sugar, baking powder, baking soda, and ¼ teaspoon salt. Cut in the ¼ cup butter till the mixture is crumbly. Make a well in the center and add milk all at once. Using a fork, stir just till dough clings together. On a lightly floured surface, knead dough gently for 10 to 12 strokes. Roll or pat dough into a 12 x 8-inch rectangle. Combine walnuts, the 3 tablespoons brown sugar, and cinnamon; brush dough with the 1 tablespoon melted butter and sprinkle with nut mixture. Roll up jelly-roll style, starting from one of the short sides. Seal edge. With a sharp knife, cut into eight 1-inch thick slices. Set aside.

Filling: in a large saucepan stir together the ⅔ cup brown sugar, cornstarch and lemon peel. Add peaches and ⅔ cup water. Cook and stir till bubbly. Transfer to a 12 x 7½ x 2-inch baking dish. Arrange biscuit slices, cut side down, on HOT filling. Bake, in a 400 degree oven about 25 minutes or till biscuit slices are golden. Serve warm with Sour Cream Topping or ice cream. Yield: 8 servings.

Courtesy of Dickey Farms, Musella, Georgia, "The Sweetest Peaches in the South"

COBBLER

CRUST

3 cups flour
3 teaspoons salt
1¼ cups Crisco
⅔ cup cold water

FILLING

4 cups peaches (including juice or any fruit)
3 cups water
2⅓ cups sugar
¾ stick butter
⅓ cup sugar

Crust: Preheat oven to 375 degrees. Mix flour and salt. Cut in Crisco. Let sit 10 minutes. Add water. Mix to form dough. Roll out over bottom and part way up sides of dish. Cook bottom layer about 10 minutes at 375 degrees.

Filling: Mix peaches and water and sugar. Pour over bottom crust. Dot with butter. For lattice, cut strips of dough 1½-inches wide and weave. Sprinkle ⅓ cup sugar over top dough. Bake 45 minutes at 375 degrees.

Darla Savage www.stratfordjelly.com

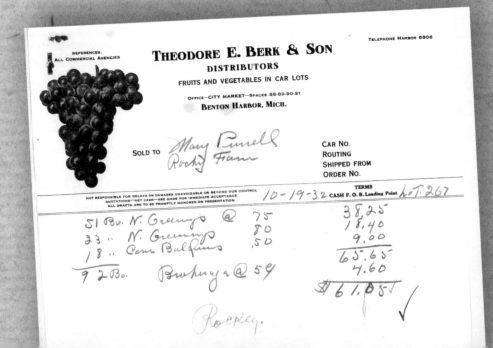

PEACH BLUEBERRY COBBLER

FILLING

- 3 cups ½-inch thick slices of peeled, pitted ripe peaches, about 5
- 1 cup fresh blueberries
- 2 tablespoons lemon juice
- ½ cup sugar
- 2 tablespoons cornstarch
- 2 tablespoons margarine melted

TOPPING

- ⅔ cup flour
- 1 tablespoon sugar
- 1 teaspoon baking powder
- ⅛ teaspoon salt
- 2 tablespoons margarine, melted
- ¼ cup sour cream
- 1 tablespoon milk
- ¼ cup sugar

Filling: Butter a 9-inch square baking dish; mix together peaches, blueberries, and lemon juice in a large bowl. Stir together sugar and cornstarch in a small bowl. Add to fruit mixture, toss together and mix well. Pour into prepared pan. Drizzle evenly with melted butter.

Topping: Stir together flour, sugar, baking powder and salt in a large bowl. Stir together melted margarine and sour cream in a small bowl. Make a well in the center of the dry ingredients, pour the sour cream mixture into the well. Stir until mix forms dough. Roll dough out on floured surface to ⅓-inch thickness. Cut out with 2½-inch round cookie cutter. Arrange cut outs evenly over fruit. Brush cut outs with milk. Sprinkle with sugar. Bake at 375 degrees for 30–35 minutes or until cut outs are golden brown and fruit filling is bubbly. Transfer to wire rack to cool.

Cecelia Drake, Glad Peach Bake Fest Winner, Coloma, Michigan

QUICK PEACH COBBLER

    4 tablespoons margarine
10– 20 ounces of sliced peaches
    1 cup sugar, divided
    ½ cup water
    ½ cup flour
    1½ teaspoons baking powder
    ½ teaspoon salt
    ½ cup milk

Preheat oven to 375 degrees. Place margarine in baking dish and melt in oven. Heat peaches, ½ cup sugar, and ½ cup water in saucepan until the sugar is dissolved. Bring to a boil. Mix flour, baking powder, salt, reminaing ½ cup sugar, and milk together in mixing bowl and stir until smooth. Set aside. Remove baking dish from oven when the margarine has melted. Add flour mixture, then peach mixture. Bake 20 to 30 minutes at 375 degrees. Crust will rise to the top and brown.

PEACH BETTY

    1½ pounds (46-ounce can) sliced peaches with syrup
    2 cups soft bread crumbs
    ¼ cup light brown sugar
    ½ teaspoon lemon juice
    2 tablespoons butter

Preheat oven to 375 degrees. Put half of the peaches in a baking dish, add half of the bread crumbs, then rest of peaches and bread crumbs. Add brown sugar and lemon juice and dot with butter. Cover and bake 30 minutes in a preheated 375 degree oven. Uncover the last 10 minutes to brown.

Thanks to Mrs. Paul Fast, Hooker, Oklahoma

PEACH OR APPLE STRUDEL

     4 cups cooking apples or sliced peaches
     1 teaspoon cinnamon
     1 teaspoon salt
     ¼ cup water
     ¾ cup flour
     1 cup sugar
     ⅓ cup butter or margarine

Preheat oven to 350 degrees. Combine fruit, cinnamon, salt, and water in a 10 x 6-inch buttered baking dish. In a separate bowl, combine flour, sugar and butter until mixture is crumbly. Spread topping over fruit. Bake in preheated 350 degree oven for 40–50 minutes. This is great plain or topped with whipped cream or quality vanilla ice cream. Serves 6.

Thanks to Bettye J. Knott, Waxahachie, Texas

PEACH CRUNCH

     ½ cup crushed gingersnap cookies*
     2 tablespoons chopped pecans
     2 tablespoons butter, melted
     1 tablespoon brown sugar
     8 large ripe peach halves, drained and peeled
     1 tablespoon fresh lemon juice
     ¼ cup orange juice
        Vanilla ice cream

Preheat oven to 350 degrees. In a chilled medium bowl, combine gingersnaps, pecans, melted butter and brown sugar. Mix thoroughly and set aside. Arrange peach halves, cut side up, in a 15 x 10 x 2-inch baking pan. Combine lemon and orange juice and drizzle over peaches. Spoon cookie mixture over peaches. Bake in preheated oven for 20 minutes. Serve a la mode in dessert dishes with vanilla ice cream. Serves 8.

*To prepare cookie crumbs, place gingersnaps into a zipper bag and roll over the bag with a rolling pin until desired consistency is reached.

NAVAJO PEACH APPLE CRISP

FILLING

- 4⅔ cups peaches, sliced and peeled (fresh or frozen)
- 3½ cups sliced peeled Granny Smith apples
- 1 tablespoon vanilla extract
- ½ cup honey
- 2 tablespoons peach brandy or plain brandy
- ½ teaspoon cinnamon

TOPPING

- 1 cup all-purpose flour
- ½ cup packed brown sugar
- ¼ teaspoon salt
- 6 tablespoons margarine
- 4 tablespoons pine nuts

Preheat oven to 375 degrees. Spray a 13 x 9-inch pan with cooking spray. Combine filling ingredients and pour into prepared pan. For topping: combine flour, sugar, and salt in a small bowl. Cut in margarine until mixture resembles coarse meal. Stir in pine nuts. Sprinkle over peach mixture. Bake at 375 degrees for 30 minutes or until lightly browned and bubbly. Serves 12.

Kathleen Parrent, Glad Peach Bake Fest Winner, Coloma, Michigan

Tree Mendus Fruit Farm began in the 1920's in when an enterprising young man sold some of his fresh Jonathan apples to a young lady with sparkling eyes. When William and Leone Teichman married two years later, they planted their dreams of growing sweet, juicy fruit on 160 acres near Eau Claire, Michigan. They christened their new farm Skyline Orchards. Because their romance sparked over a basket of Jonathan apples, William's first planting was 15 acres of this one variety. It was unheard of at that time to plant so much of one type of apple. Two rows of those Jonathan apples still exist on the farm and can be seen while touring the grounds. Skyline Orchards has evolved to encompass over 450 acres now known as Tree-Mendus Fruit Farm, managed by a family four generations strong. When Herb and Liz Teichman purchased the farm from his parents in 1969, it was their goal to have enough land to operate a recreational and "pick your own" farm. That tradition continues today with the family continuing to grow fine apples, cherries, apricots, peaches, nectarines, plums, pears and raspberries.

Tree-Mendus Fruit Farm has been host to many family activities for over 25 years, including the popular International Cherry Pit Spitting Championship, held every year on the first Saturday in July. It's the only Cherry Pit Spitting Contest recognized by the Guinness Book of World Records. Their philosophy is: "Spit your pit in public with only a minimal loss of dignity while gaining fame."

Visit their web site: http://www.treemendus-fruit.com/index.html, for driving directions and an event calendar. They are located in Eau Claire, Michigan and are open from June through Labor Day, with limited off-season hours available as well.

PEACH OATMEAL COOKIE CRISP

½ cup packed brown sugar
¼ cup flour
¼ teaspoon ground cinnamon
¼ cup unsalted butter, cold
6 oatmeal cookies, broken into small pieces
5 medium fresh peaches, peeled and sliced (4 cups)
2 teaspoons lemon juice
2 tablespoons sugar or Splenda®
2 teaspoons cornstarch
Pinch salt

Preheat oven to 350 degrees. Combine brown sugar, flour, and cinnamon in bowl. Cut in butter until crumbly. Stir in cookie pieces. Place peaches into a separate bowl and add lemon juice, sugar, cornstarch and salt. Mix well. Pour into an ungreased 9-inch pie plate. Sprinkle topping over fruit. Bake for 30 minutes. Serve warm with ice cream. Serves 6.

Thanks to Bettye J. Knott, Waxahachie, Texas

PEACH CHERRY TORT

Elegant open faced tort.

1 cup Michigan dried cherries
½ cup granulated sugar
2 tablespoons flour
½ teaspoon ground cinnamon
¼ teaspoon salt
4 large ripe peaches, sliced with skins
1 tablespoon lemon juice
1 (9-inch) unbaked pie shell

Preheat oven to 425 degrees. Combine cherries, sugar, flour, cinnamon, and salt. Mix with peaches and lemon juice. Place 9-inch round pie shell onto a rimmed baking sheet. Mound fruit in center of dough, leaving a ½-inch border. Fold edge of dough up around fruit, gently pleating and pressing dough against fruit.

Bake in a preheated 425 degree oven for 10 minutes. Reduce heat to 350 degrees and bake 25 minutes until crust is golden brown. Juices may seep out onto pan. Cool on pan. With a large spatula, carefully transfer tort to a platter and dust with powdered sugar just before serving. Serves 8.

PEACH TART

1 cup all-purpose flour
¼ teaspoon salt
¼ cup butter
4–5 tablespoons cold water
1 (8-ounce) package fat free cream cheese, softened
¼ cup sugar or sugar substitute equal to ¼ cup
1 teaspoon vanilla
4 or 5 peeled peaches, sliced or 1 (16-ounce) package frozen peach slices, thawed and drained
½ cup blueberries
½ cup low-calorie apricot spread

Preheat oven to 400 degrees. Pastry: In a medium bowl, combine flour and salt. Using a pastry blender, cut in butter until pieces are the size of a pea. Sprinkle 1 tablespoon cold water over a portion of the mixture. Toss with a fork. Repeat until moisture is absorbed. Form a ball. Set aside. On a lightly floured surface, flatten pastry. Roll into a 12-inch circle. Ease pastry into a 10-inch tart pan with a removable bottom, being careful not to stretch pastry. Press pastry about ½-inch up the sides of pan. Prick the bottom well with a fork. Bake at 450 degrees for 12–15 minutes or until golden brown. Cool on wire rack. Remove sides of tart pan.

In a medium bowl, combine cream cheese, sugar substitute or sugar and vanilla. Beat with an electric mixer until smooth and then spread over cooked pastry. Arrange peaches over cream cheese layer. Sprinkle with blueberries.

In a small saucepan, heat apricot spread until melted. Spoon melted spread over fruit. Chill for at least 2 hours and up to 3 hours. Serves 12.

GEORGIA PEACH TART

1 cup all-purpose flour
¼ teaspoon salt
¼ cup chilled margarine
2 to 4 tablespoons cold water
4 ounces light cream cheese, softened
2 tablespoons sugar
½ teaspoon vanilla extract
4 or 5 medium Georgia peaches, peeled and
    sliced
½ cup low-calorie apple jelly

Preheat oven to 450 degrees. For pastry, in a mixing bowl combine the flour and salt. Cut in the chilled margarine until pieces are the size of small peas. Sprinkle 1 tablespoon of the cold water over part of the mixture. Toss with a fork. Push to the side of the bowl. Repeat until all of the mixture is moistened. Form into a ball. On a lightly floured surface roll pastry into a 12-inch circle. Wrap pastry around the rolling pin. Ease into an 11-inch flan pan. Do not stretch. Press pastry up the sides of the pan. Trim pastry even with the top of the pan. Prick bottom of crust well with tines of a fork. Bake in 450 degree oven for 10 to 12 minutes or until golden. Cool on wire rack. Meanwhile, in a small mixing bowl stir together cream cheese, sugar, and vanilla until smooth. Spread atop cooled crust. Arrange peach slices in circles atop cheese mixture. In a small saucepan heat apple jelly until melted. Spoon over peaches. Chill for at least 2 hours or up to 8 hours. Yield: 12 servings

Courtesy of Dickey Farms, Musella, Georgia, "The Sweetest Peaches in the South"

PEACH ALMOND TART

1 (9-inch) pie shell
1 (14-ounce) can Eagle Brand® condensed milk
1 (8-ounce) carton sour cream
2 tablespoons lemon juice
1 teaspoon almond extract
1 (21-ounce) can peach pie filling
1 small bag almonds, lightly toasted

Preheat oven to 350 degrees. Bake pie shell according to package directions. In a medium bowl, combine condensed milk, sour cream, lemon juice, and almond extract. Mix well. Set aside. Reserve 6 peach slices, spread remaining pie filling on bottom of prepared pie shell. Pour sour cream mixture over pie filling. Top with reserved peach slices and almonds. Bake at 350 degrees for 30 minutes or until set. Cool, then chill in refrigerator. Keep any leftovers in refrigerator.

Ashley Hert, Glad Peach Bake Fest Winner, Coloma, Michigan

FRESH GEORGIA PEACH TARTS

4 cups sliced fresh Georgia peaches
¾ cup sugar
2 teaspoons fresh lemon juice
1 tablespoon cornstarch
4 (5-inch) tart shells, baked

Combine peaches, sugar, and lemon juice in bowl; mix well. Let stand for 20 minutes. Drain, reserving juice. Add enough water to reserved juice to measure 1 cup. Pour juice into saucepan. Stir in cornstarch gradually. Cook until transparent, stirring constantly. Cool. Spoon peaches into tart shells. Pour juice syrup over peaches. Chill until glaze is set. Garnish with clusters of dark grapes. Yield: 4 tarts.

Courtesy of Dickey Farms, Musella, Georgia , The Sweetest Peaches in the South"

. PEACH TARTS

Cook 2 cups peaches cut in eighths, 1
cup sugar, 1 tablespoon lemon juice,
1 tablespoon butter, and a few grains
salt, until peaches are tender. Cool
and fill tarts.

PEACH TARTLETS

1 *sheet frozen puff pastry, thaw on counter*
   for 30 minutes
3 *slightly under ripe peaches, peeled and*
   sliced into ⅛-inch slices
3 *tablespoons unsalted butter, melted*
2 *tablespoons sugar or Splenda®*

Preheat oven to 375 degrees. Lin a large baking sheet with parchment paper. Unfold pastry onto lightly floured board. Roll dough to ¼-inch thickness. Cut four 6-inch circles from dough. Place circles on parchment papered sheet and place in refrigerator to chill. Remove baking sheet from refrigerator. Using three-fourths of a sliced peach, fan slices on dough circles. Leave a pie crust border. Brush with melted butter and sprinkle with sugar or Splenda®. Bake 20–25 minutes until golden brown.

FRESH GEORGIA PEACH DUMPLINGS

- 1 cup dark corn syrup
- ½ cup water
- ¼ cup lemon juice
- 1 teaspoon grated lemon peel
- 2 tablespoons butter or margarine
- 2 cups all-purpose flour
- 2 teaspoons baking powder
- ½ teaspoon salt
- ½ cup shortening
- ¾ cup whole milk
- 2½ cups sliced Georgia peaches
- ½ cup sugar
- ¼ teaspoon cinnamon
- ¼ teaspoon nutmeg

Preheat oven to 425 degrees. Combine corn syrup, water, lemon juice and lemon peel in a sauce pan. Bring to a boil and simmer 10 minutes. Add butter and remove syrup mixture from heat. Mix flour, baking powder and salt together. Cut in shortening. Add milk and stir just until moistened. Roll out ½-inch thick and cut into eight 5-inch squares. Combine peaches, sugar, cinnamon and nutmeg. Place 2 tablespoons of the peach mixture onto each square. Fold corners to center and pinch edges to seal. Arrange pouches in a greased 8 x 12-inch baking dish. Pour syrup mixture over dumplings, moistening each. Bake at 425 degrees for 10 minutes. Reduce heat to 350 degrees and bake 30 minutes longer. Serve warm. Yield: 8 servings.

Courtesy of Dickey Farms, Musella, Georgia, "The Sweetest Peaches in the South"

CORNFLAKE RING WITH PEACHES AND CREAM

RING

- 1 cup packed brown sugar
- ⅓ cup milk
- 3 tablespoons butter
- 2 tablespoons light corn syrup
- 4 cup cornflakes
- ¾ cup toasted almonds, chopped

TOPPING

- 4 cups sliced fresh South Carolina peaches
- 1 tablespoon brown sugar
- ½ cup whipping cream
- 2 teaspoons granulated sugar
- ½ teaspoon vanilla extract
- 2 tablespoons sliced almonds

In 2-quart saucepan, combine sugar, milk, butter and corn syrup. Boil to soft ball stage (238 degrees). Toss cornflakes and almonds in a large buttered bowl. Pour hot syrup over all and toss quickly. Pack into well-buttered 8-inch ring mold. Set aside 10 minutes. Run knife around edge and unmold onto plate. Cool before filling.

Toss peaches with brown sugar. Chill. In a separate bowl, whip cream to soft peaks. Beat in sugar and vanilla until stiff. Fold in peaches. Fill ring with some of peaches and cream, sprinkled with almonds. To serve: Cut ring into ½-inch slices. Serve 2 to 3 slices topped with additional peaches and cream. Serves 6–8.

Courtesy of South Carolina Peach Council

PEACH DUMPLINGS

Roll out pastry dough in rounds about the size of fruit plates. In the center of each, place a whole peeled peach. Sprinkle the peach with a mixture of sugar, cinnamon, and a few grains of salt. Dot the fruit with butter. Lift up and press together the edges of the dough together. Place in greased muffin tins and bake in a moderate oven (350–375 degree) for 30 minutes. Serve hot with hard or liquid sauce.

CASH FARMS

The Cash Farms began as land grant properties back in the 1700's. In 1925 the family planted their first peach trees. Tucked into the rolling hills of the Piedmont are the Klein Cash family, the present owners of the well known Cash Farms.

We talked about the past with the huge acreage devoted to peaches, the fleet of trucks, the masses of employees, the continual buying of new equipment. Times have changed and the need to diversify changed with the times. Cash Farms continue to raise their well known peaches along with strawberries, cattle, corn and cotton. To extend their season, they now use their packing shed for repackaging Peruvian onions that come to them by containers and will be sold to other companies.

Klein and his wife Vickie are so happy to have their oldest son Chad and daughter Cindy active in the business. They are equally as happy for their youngest son who has felt the call to the ministry. If you listen closely, you hear the voices of children; those are the voices of the five grandchildren that work and play at the farm each day.

PEACH FRENCH TOAST DESSERT

Pam spray
- 8 *large ripe peaches, peeled and sliced*
- 1 *tablespoon lemon juice*
- 1 *cup raw sugar, divided*
- ⅓ *cup all-purpose flour*
- 1 *teaspoon fresh grated orange rind*
- ⅓ *cup fresh orange juice*
- ¼ *cup butter, melted*
- ¼ *teaspoon ground cinnamon*
- 3 *large egg whites*
- 8 *slices white wheat or white multigrain bread*
- 2 *tablespoons raw or granulated sugar*

Preheat oven to 350 degrees. Coat a 13 x 9-inch baking pan with Pam spray. Add peaches, lemon juice, ¾ cup raw sugar and flour. Let stand for 30 minutes, stirring occasionally. In a large chilled bowl, combine ¼ cup raw sugar, orange rind, orange juice, butter, cinnamon and egg whites. Whisk until smooth. Remove crust from bread with a knife. Cut each slice of bread into 2 triangles. Dip bread in orange juice mixture and then arrange bread on top of peach mixture. Sprinkle bread with raw sugar. Bake at 350 degrees for 50 minutes.

GEORGIA PEACH DELIGHT

- 2½ *cups self-rising flour*
- 2 *sticks butter, softened*
- 1 *cup chopped nuts*
- 1 *(8-ounce) package cream cheese, room temperature*
- 2½ *cups powdered sugar, sifted*
- 1 *(8-ounce) tub frozen whipped topping*
- 4 *cups sliced Georgia peaches*
- 1 *cup sugar*
- 1 *cup water*
- 4 *tablespoons plain flour*
- 4 *tablespoons peach gelatin*

Preheat oven to 350 degrees. Mix self-rising flour, butter and nuts well with spoon and spread in 13 x 9-inch pan. Bake at 350 degrees for 20–25 minutes. Set aside to cool. Beat together cream cheese, powdered sugar, and whipped topping with electric mixer and spread on crust. Add peaches. Mix sugar, water, plain flour and peach gelatin and cook over medium heat until thick, stirring constantly. Cool slightly and pour over peaches, evenly coating all. Refrigerate.

Courtesy of Dickey Farms, Musella, Georgia, "The Sweetest Peaches in the South"

PEACH CREAM CHEESE DESSERT

¾ cup flour

1 (4-serving) package vanilla pudding mix, NOT instant

1 teaspoon baking powder

1 beaten egg

½ cup milk

3 tablespoons melted margarine

1 (16-ounce) can Georgia peaches, drained and chopped, reserve the juice

1 (8-ounce) package cream cheese

½ cup plus 1 tablespoon white sugar, separated

½ teaspoon cinnamon

Mix flour, pudding and baking powder together. Combine egg, milk and margarine; add to dry ingredients. Pour into a greased 8-inch square pan. Add peaches. Beat together cream cheese, ½ cup sugar and peach juice. Pour over the top. Then sprinkle with 1 tablespoon sugar and cinnamon. Bake at 350 degrees for 45 minutes.

Courtesy of Dickey Farms, Musella, Georgia, "The Sweetest Peaches in the South"

CREAM PUFFS

PUFFS

1 cup water

1 stick butter

1 cup flour

4 eggs

FILLING

½ cup whipping cream

1 (4-serving) box instant vanilla pudding

2 cups milk

Peach slices

Preheat oven to 400 degrees. Place water and butter in a pot and boil until butter melts. Add flour and stir until dough leaves the side of the pot. Remove from heat, beat in 1 egg at a time, stir only until eggs are well combined. Bake for 40 minutes in a 400 degree oven. Cool. For filling: beat whipping cream and combine with pudding and milk. When cool, fill puffs with a heaping tablespoon of filling. Place 2 to 3 peach slices in each puff. Sprinkle with confectioners' sugar.

Wanda Zurek, Glad Peach Bake Fest Winner, Coloma, Michigan

RAW EGG ON TOAST

Slice of low fat pound cake
Reduced calorie whipped topping in can
Half of a South Carolina peach

Place half of peach on a slice of pound cake. Spray whipped topping around peach. Serves 1.

Courtesy of YMCA of Uptown Columbia and South Carolina Peach Council

FRUIT CUP

Many combinations of fruit, fresh or canned, may be used for a fruit cup. Use brightly colored fruits or colors that blend or contrast pleasantly. Combine acid fruits with sweet and firm with juicy kinds, a good combination is peaches, raspberries and pineapple. Cut large fruits into small attractive pieces, mix lightly so that they keep their shape, sweeten slightly, chill before serving, and garnish the individual servings with sprigs of mint.

NON FAT NATURAL PEACH DESSERT

2 *tablespoons fresh orange juice*
2 *tablespoons peach liqueur*
2 *tablespoons honey*
4 *large ripe peaches*
2 *cups cantaloupe*
2 *cups honey dew melon*

Mix first three ingredients in a chilled small bowl. Slice peaches in wedges and dice melons. Gently mix peaches and melons together in a separate bowl. Pour syrup over fruit and mix gently. Refrigerate in non-metal bowl for one hour. Serve over yogurt, ice cream or by itself. Serves 8.

CALIFORNIA CLING PEACH CHARLOTTE

  2 *sticks (8-ounces) unsalted butter, at room temperature*
  1 *cup sugar, preferably superfine*
  5 *tablespoons Frangelico almond liqueur, Grand Marnier, or syrup from the peaches (if using peach syrup, add ½ teaspoon almond extract)*
1½ *cups finely ground almonds (reserve 1 tablespoon for garnish)*
  2 *cups whipping cream*
  1 *tablespoon sugar*
  1 *teaspoon vanilla extract*
  3 *(15-ounce) cans California cling peach slices, well drained (reserve 5 slices for garnish)*

Line the bottom of the spring form pan with a circle of waxed paper. Using an electric mixer, cream the butter and superfine sugar together for 4 or 5 minutes, until pale and airy. Add the Frangelico almond liqueur, Grand Marnier or reserved peach syrup and almond extract. Continue to beat for a few more minutes until the sugar has nearly dissolved. Blend in the almonds. Reserve. Whip the cream with the sugar and vanilla until it just holds very soft peaks.

Fold the lightly whipped cream completely into the almond mixture.

Cover the bottom of the spring form pan with one-third of the almond cream. Arrange half of the peach slices in a sunburst pattern on the almond cream. Cover with another one-third of the almond cream. Repeat with another layer of peach slices and cover with the remaining almond cream. Firmly tap the filled pan onto work surface to settle the mixture and remove any air pockets that may have formed. Cover with plastic wrap and refrigerate for at least 5 hours or overnight. The California Cling Peach Charlotte may be prepared a day in advance to this point.

To Serve: Remove the plastic wrap and run a knife around the edge of the pan. Unlatch the spring form pan leaving the ring in place. Place the selected serving plate upside down over the mold and reverse the finished charlotte onto the plate. Remove the ring and the bottom of the pan. Remove the waxed paper. Garnish with reserved peach slices and sprinkle with the reserved ground almonds. Refrigerate until ready to serve. For best results, slice with a damp knife. Makes one (8½-inch) charlotte.

Created for The California Cling Peach Board by Gary Jenanyan. Photo courtesy California Cling Peach Board.

PALMETTO PEACH PIZZA

CRUST

2   cups unbleached flour
2   teaspoons baking powder
⅓   cup butter
2   tablespoons yeast
¾   cup WARM water
2   tablespoons maple syrup

FILLING

2   pounds fresh South Carolina peaches, sliced
⅓   cup fresh lemon juice
¼   cup unbleached flour
¼   teaspoon nutmeg
¼   cup butter
¼   cup maple syrup
¼   cup graham cracker crumbs

Preheat oven to 350 degrees. For the crust, combine flour and baking powder; cut in butter. Dissolve yeast in warm water and maple syrup. Let sit for 5 minutes and stir into flour mixture, blending well. Turn onto floured board and knead lightly for 5 minutes, adding flour as necessary. Let dough rest for 10 minutes. Using a floured rolling pin, roll out the dough to fit either a cookie sheet or round 10-inch pizza pan. Transfer dough to oiled pan. If the dough is too sticky to lift from board to pan, then, using your hands, pat the dough into the pan you will use. Pinch up edges 1-inch all the way around cookie sheet or pizza pan to form rim. Slice peaches and pour lemon juice on top; set aside. Cut together flour, nutmeg, butter, maple syrup and graham cracker crumbs. Spread and sprinkle half of it over the bottom of the pizza dough. Arrange the peach slices on the dough, in layers if necessary. Sprinkle remaining mixture on top of peaches. Bake at 350 degrees 25–30 minutes. Serve warm or cooled.

Courtesy of South Carolina Peach Council

GEORGIA PEACHY PIZZA

½ cup margarine or butter

1 cup all-purpose flour

¼ cup sifted confectioners' sugar

2 tablespoons granulated sugar

2 tablespoons cornstarch

⅛ teaspoon ground mace

⅔ cup orange juice

½ cup currant jelly

4 medium Georgia peaches, peeled and sliced

1 cup sliced strawberries

½ cup blueberries

½ cup seedless green grapes, halved

Preheat oven to 350 degrees. For crust, in a small mixer bowl, beat margarine or butter with an electric mixer on medium-high speed for 30 seconds. Gradually add flour and confectioners' sugar until combined. Pat dough evenly over bottom and up sides of a 12-inch pizza pan. Bake at 350 degrees for 10 to 12 minutes or until golden; cool on a wire rack. Meanwhile, for glaze, stir together the granulated sugar, cornstarch, and mace in a medium saucepan. Stir in orange juice and jelly. Cook and stir over medium heat until thickened and bubbly. Cook and stir 2 minutes more. Cool slightly. Spread half of the glaze (about ⅔ cup) onto cooled crust. Arrange peach slices around edge of crust, then arrange strawberries, working toward center of crust. Sprinkle all with blueberries and grapes. Drizzle remaining glaze over fruit. Chill until needed. Cut into wedges to serve. Yield: 12 servings.

Courtesy of Dickey Farms, Musella, Georgia, "The Sweetest Peaches in the South"

PEACH ENCHILADAS

2 (8-ounce) tubes crescent rolls

2 sticks butter

4 firm South Carolina peaches, peeled and quartered

1½ cups sugar

1 teaspoon cinnamon

1 (12-ounce) can citrus flavored soda-like Mountain Dew

Preheat oven to 350 degrees. Let Mom or Dad peel and quarter peaches. Melt butter. Add sugar and cinnamon. Unroll crescents and place peach quarters in each one. Roll up from large to small end. Place in a 12 x 10 x 2-inch pan coated with nonstick spray. Pour butter mixture over rolls and pour citrus flavored soda on top. Bake at 350 degrees for 45 minutes. Serves 16.

Courtesy of Mac's Pride Peaches in McBee, SC and South Carolina Peach Council

PEACH PRETZEL DELIGHT

CRUST

4 cups crushed pretzels

1 stick butter, melted

3 tablespoons sugar

Mix together and press into a 13 x 9-inch pan, bake 15 minutes at 350 degrees, allow to cool.

FILLING

8 ounces heavy cream whipped with sugar

2 (8-ounce) packages cream cheese, softened

¼ cup sugar

TOPPING

4–5 cups of fresh chopped South Carolina peaches, sugar to sweeten

1 (4-serving) box peach Jell-O®

1 jar caramel ice cream topping

Whip cream with enough sugar to sweeten, set aside. Beat cream cheese & sugar until incorporated, fold in whipped cream and pour over the pretzel crust. Mix chopped peaches with dry Jell-O® and set aside for 5 minutes. Mix peach mixture with caramel topping and pour over cream cheese and serve.

Courtesy of South Carolina Peach Council

PEACH CORNBREAD TRIFLE

2 pounds very ripe South Carolina peaches

¼ cup sugar

2 cups heavy cream

½ teaspoon vanilla extract

1 pound cornbread either store-bought or homemade

Score the bottom of peaches with an "X." Remove peach skins by dropping them into a pot of simmering water for 30 to 60 seconds. Remove the peaches, set aside to cool in a bowl of ice water and then peel off the loosened skins. Remove the pits from the peaches and then finely chop the flesh. Put the chopped peaches in a bowl. Pour the cream into another large mixing bowl. Add a ¼ cup sugar and the vanilla extract. Whip into soft peaks. Cut the corn bread into thin slices. Layer the bottom of a clear glass trifle or other serving bowl with a third of the cornbread. Add a third of the peaches on top of the cornbread and then a third of the whipped cream on top of that. Repeat the layers two more times and crumble the final layer of the cornbread on top. Refrigerate and serve cold.

Courtesy of South Carolina Peach Council

PEACH MELBA

This classic dessert was named for Australian opera singer and food enthusiast, Dame Nellie Melba by French chef Auguste Escoffier. Often called the greatest chef who ever lived, Escoffier was working at the Ritz Hotel in London in the early 1900's, the period when Melba performed at Covent Garden opera house. Escoffier also created Melba toast—bread heated in a low oven until golden brown and very brittle—in Melba's honor.

4 large ripe peaches, blanched
1 cup sugar syrup
1 teaspoon vanilla extract
1 quart quality vanilla ice cream
3 cups melba sauce

Cut the peaches in half and remove pods. Combine syrup and vanilla in a saucepan and boil for 5 minutes. Poach peaches in syrup for 10 minutes, then remove from syrup. Refrigerate peaches for 20 minutes. Place scoops of ice cream into 8 compotes, then place peach halves over ice cream, cut side down. Top with melba sauce. Garnish with sprigs of fresh mint.

MELBA SAUCE

1 quart fresh red raspberries, pureed
¼ cup currant jelly
2 teaspoons corn starch
1 tablespoon Baileys Bristol Cream (optional)

Combine raspberries and jelly in a sauce pan over low heat and stir until jelly is melted. Dissolve cornstarch in 2 tablespoons of water and add to the raspberry mixture, stirring constantly until mixture is clear. Add Baileys. Makes 3 cups of sauce.

Thanks to Myrtle Heyn Totzke

SUGAR SYRUP
Sugar Syrup to be used on sweet breads, peach melba or other desserts.

3 cups water
4 cups sugar

Place water and sugar into a pot over low heat, cook until sugar dissolves. Bring syrup to a boil, then reduce heat to low for 4 minutes. Chill, pour into jars or bottles and store.
Courtesy of The Creative Cookery Course

PETITE PEACH MELBA

4 tablespoons granulated sugar

4 tablespoons butter

½ cup packed brown sugar

4 tablespoons Florida orange juice

4 tablespoons fresh lemon juice

6 ripe medium peaches, peeled, pitted and sliced

2 cups fresh raspberries, drained (if using frozen fruit, be sure to thaw and drain)

½ cup peach brandy

Homemade vanilla ice cream, optional

Melt butter in a medium saucepan. Add sugar, brown sugar, and orange juice. Stir syrup over medium heat until sugar is dissolved and syrup starts to bubble. Sprinkle peaches with lemon juice. Add sliced peaches to mixture; stir gently. Turn heat to low, simmer uncovered for 5 minutes until mixture bubbles. Spoon in raspberries and brandy; immediately remove from heat. Scoop ice cream into dessert dishes and ladle hot fruit on top. Serves 8.

STUFFED PEACH

1 large fully ripe freestone peach

3–5 fresh raspberries

1½ tablespoons orange juice or optional orange flavored liqueur

Cut an almond shape around the stem at the end of the peach through to the stone. Now insert a skewer at the opposite end and push the stone out the hole you cut in the other end. Insert the raspberries into the cavity. Carefully rub the entire peach skin with the back of a spoon to loosen the skin and then slip it off. Place the peach in a fruit compote, spoon the orange juice over the peach, adding fine quality vanilla ice cream, yogurt or a little cream.

Lee Totzke

SWEET PULP

6 large ripe peaches
½ cup confectioners' sugar
3 large eggs
Whipped cream
Red raspberries (optional)

Peel, halve and remove stones from peaches; put them through a sieve and add sugar. Beat the whites of the eggs and add to peach mixture, stir until thick and smooth. Pour into a decorative chilled mold, keep it chilled on ice. Serve with dollop of whipped cream. Garnish with three red raspberries per serving.

PEACHES AND RASPBERRIES

8 ripe firm peaches
Simple syrup (2 cups sugar and 2 cups water)
⅓ cup bourbon
½ pint red raspberries

Boil sugar and water together for 10 minutes. Peel peaches, dip into syrup till just tender. Add bourbon. Quickly dip raspberries in syrup and spoon over peaches. Serve cold. Serves 8.

Private Mailing Card.

BENTON HARBOR, MICHIGAN

PLACE THE POSTAGE STAMP HERE

COPYRIGHT APPLIED FOR

WHO GETS THE LOAD?

PETERS & ALGER

PEACH CARDINAL

6 *cups water*
2 *cups granulated sugar*
8 *large ripe firm peaches, peeled, halved and stoned*
1 *(4-inch) piece of vanilla*

In a heavy 4-quart saucepan make a simple syrup. Boil water and sugar at high heat for 4 minutes, continually stirring until sugar dissolves. Reduce heat to low, add peaches and vanilla and poach uncovered at this very low temperature for 15 minutes until tender. Chill peaches in syrup.

SAUCE CARDINAL

2 *(10-ounce) packages frozen red raspberries, defrost and drain*
2 *tablespoons superfine sugar*
1 *tablespoon Kirsch*

Place raspberries into a blender and totally puree. Pour puree into a small, chilled mixing bowl. Add sugar and Kirsch to raspberries. Pour puree into a container, cover tightly and refrigerate.

CREAM OF LACE

¾ *cup chilled heavy cream*
2 *tablespoons superfine sugar*
1 *tablespoon vanilla extract*
Defrosted frozen raspberries for garnish

With an electric beater and a chilled mixing bowl, whip cream until it thickens. Spoon sugar and vanilla into mixture; continue beating until the cream holds the peaks on the beater.

To serve: using a slotted spoon place the chilled peaches into eight dessert dishes. Sugar syrup can be saved to poach more peaches. Cover each peach with the Sauce Cardinal and add your personal touch by decorating with cream of lace. Garnish with raspberries or something else of your choice.

Thanks to Augusta Gast Totzke

BRANDIED PEACHES AND CREAM

8 ripe firm peaches
1 tablespoon unsalted butter
1 lemon, juiced
8 tablespoons brandy
2 tablespoons light brown sugar
2 teaspoons ground cinnamon

Preheat oven to 350 degrees. Cut an X on the bottom of each peach. Using a slotted spoon, place the peaches in a saucepan with enough boiling water to cover peaches. Boil for 30 seconds. Using the slotted spoon, immediately plunge peaches into ice water, drain. Peel, cut peaches into quarters and remove pit. Using a large shallow baking dish, arrange peach quarters cut side up. Dot with butter. Combine lemon juice and brandy. Pour over peaches. Sprinkle sugar and cinnamon over peaches. Bake for 20 minutes on center oven rack. Cool until just warm. Serve in a dessert dish with quality vanilla ice cream. Accent with almond slivers (optional). Serves 8.

Thanks to Grace Topp

POACHED EMPRESS PEACHES

6 large ripe peaches
Basic sugar syrup
1 vanilla pod or 1 teaspoon vanilla extract
2 cups hulled strawberries, pureed
½ cup sifter confectioners' sugar
3 tablespoons brandy
½ cup whipping cream, whipped

Place the peaches into a large saucepan and add enough boiling water to cover. Let stand for about 2 minutes, then lift the peaches out and dip into ice water. Slip the skins from the peaches and place peaches into a large saucepan. Pour enough syrup over the peaches to cover. Add vanilla pod to syrup. Simmer until peaches are just tender, turning once. Drain the peaches, reserving the vanilla pod for later use. Cool peaches, then chill. Combine strawberries, sugar and brandy, then fold in the whipped cream. Place peaches into a serving dish and spoon strawberry mixture on top. Serves 6.

LEE'S DEVINE POACHED PEACHES

1 cup sugar
2 cups water
8 large ripe firm peaches
Juice of 1 large lemon
2 vanilla pods, split
1 cup champagne

Make a simple syrup by dissolving the sugar in 2 cups of water and boiling it for 10 minutes. Set aside. Dip peaches in boiling water and remove skin easily. Place peaches close to one another in a saucepan. Drizzle lemon juice over peaches. Add the simple syrup, champagne and split vanilla pod. Bring combination to a boil and lower heat to simmer for 20 minutes, while constantly turning peaches with a large spoon.

Allow peaches to cool in their syrup and marinate for two days. Serve with a dollop of whipped cream and vanilla pods presented on top (optional). Serves 8.

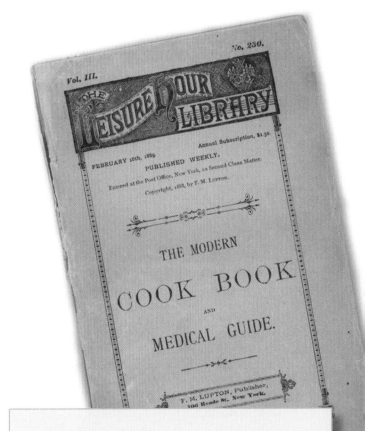

Vol. III.
No. 230.

THE LEISURE HOUR LIBRARY

FEBRUARY 16th, 1889.
Annual Subscription, $1.50.
PUBLISHED WEEKLY,
Entered at the Post Office, New York, as Second Class Matter.
Copyright, 1888, by F. M. Lupton.

THE MODERN
COOK BOOK
AND
MEDICAL GUIDE.

F. M. LUPTON, Publisher,
108 Reade St. New York.

BAKED PEACHES

Select firm ripe peaches, peel, remove the stones and place in a shallow earthenware baking dish in layers. Sprinkle the layers lightly with sugar and bake.

From: Vegetarian Cook Book
Eden Springs Israelite House of David, 1912

SUMMER PEACHES POACHED IN PINOT NOIR WINE

6 fresh ripe peaches
1 bottle Pinot Noir red wine (not expensive)
1 cup sugar
1 cinnamon stick
3 cloves
1 teaspoon ground cardamom
1 slice fresh ginger
6 white peppercorns

Plunge the peaches into boiling water for 2 minutes. Cool quickly, then peel and cut the peaches in half and discard the pit. In a wide and shallow saucepan add the wine, sugar and spices. Bring to a boil. Add the peaches (you may have to do two batches if there is not enough room.) Poach over medium heat for 5 minutes on one side. Turn over and poach another minute on the other side. Remove the peaches and let drain on a rack. Return the red wine poaching liquid to heat and reduce by one half. Refrigerate the syrup until cooled completely. Pour the chilled syrup over the peaches, cover and refrigerate. Serve chilled with crème anglaise and mint if desired. Serves 6.

Created by Vinzenz Aschbacher, Executive Pastry Chef, Charleston Grill South Carolina Peach Council

PEACHES IN MERLOT

8 large ripe, firm, cling free peaches
1 teaspoon lemon juice
2½ cups red merlot wine
1 cup granulated sugar

Peel peaches, remove stones and cut into spoon size wedges, sprinkle with lemon juice, gently mix with slotted spoon, reserve.

In a large chilled mixing bowl combine wine and sugar, stir until sugar dissolves. With a slotted spoon place peaches in sugared wine; cover and allow fruit to marinate in refrigerator for one day. Serve peaches and merlot in 8 dessert goblets or bowls.

ROASTED PEACHES

1½ cups granulated sugar
2 teaspoons vanilla extract
1 teaspoon lemon juice
8 large firm ripe peaches, halved with stones removed
1 cup water
½ cup butter, melted
Home made vanilla ice cream, optional

Preheat oven to 350 degrees. Stir sugar, vanilla, and lemon juice in a chilled mixing bowl. Spread half of mixture over the bottom of a large baking dish. Place peach halves, cut side down on top of mixture. Pour water over peaches. Cover peaches with melted butter using a brush. Coat peaches with remaining sugar mixture. Place peaches in preheated oven and roast for 15 minutes, until peaches become tender and just start to gel. Spoon juice over peaches three times while roasting.

Serve in a fruit compote with a dollop of ice cream with juices drizzled over the top.

PEACH BAKE

2 tablespoons butter
2 cups crumbled Shredded Wheat® cereal
¼ teaspoon nutmeg
½ teaspoon cinnamon
⅛ teaspoon salt
1 cup sugar
Butter for baking dish
3 cups sliced peaches
4 tablespoons lemon juice
4 tablespoons water
1 tablespoon peach liqueur (optional)

Preheat oven to 350 degrees. Melt 2 tablespoons butter in top of double boiler over boiling water. Add cereal. Stir until well blended. In a separate bowl, combine spices, salt and sugar. Set aside. Cover bottom of baking dish with butter. Spread buttered crumbs in baking dish. Add a layer of peaches. Sprinkle with sugar mixture. Add another layer of crumbs, then peaches and then sugar mixture. Make sure that sugar mixture is the top layer. Combine lemon juice, water, and liqueur and pour over crumbs. Bake for 45 minutes in a preheated 350 degree oven. May be served hot or cold.

LAZY GOURMET PEACH AMARETTI

2 *South Carolina Peaches, halved and pitted*
1 *cup crumbled amaretti cookies*
4 *tablespoons butter*
½ *cup Amaretto or Marsala*

Preheat oven to 350 degrees. Spray an 8-inch baking dish with nonstick cooking spray. Place halved pitted peaches in dish. Top with crumbled amaretti cookies. Pour Amaretto or Marsala over peaches. Top with a slice of butter. Cook until bubbly and brown. Serves 4.

Courtesy of Mouzon Taylor, hostess at the Charleston Place Hotel in Charleston, SC. Published by the South Carolina Peach Council

STEWED PEACHES

¼ *cup sugar*
¾ *cup water*
4 *whole cloves*
1½ *pounds peaches, peeled and halved*

About 20 minutes before serving: In medium saucepan over medium heat, heat sugar, water and cloves to boiling. Add peaches; return to boiling. Reduce heat to low; cover and simmer 10 minutes or until tender. Makes 6 servings.

SPANISH PEACHES

1 *quart peach halves*
3 *tablespoons dark brown sugar*
2 *tablespoons lime juice*
¼ *cup dry sherry (optional)*
1 *tablespoon grated lime peel*

Early in day: Peal and halve peaches, capturing approximately ½ cup of the juice. In small saucepan over medium heat, heat reserved peach juice, sugar and lime juice for 5 minutes. Stir in sherry. Meanwhile, place peach halves, flat side down, in dish; pour syrup over them and sprinkle with lime peel. Refrigerate until serving time. Makes 8–9 servings.

BROWN SUGARED PEACHES

1 (16-ounce) can peach halves, or fresh
  peaches with ⅛ cup sugar syrup
3 tablespoons brown sugar
2 teaspoons lemon juice
2 tablespoons rum

Drain peach halves, saving juice. In a medium sauce pan, combine saved juice, brown sugar and lemon juice. Cook and stir over low heat until sugar is dissolved and syrup is well heated. Add rum and gently spoon peach halves into the syrup. Cook for about 3 minutes. To serve, spoon peach halves and syrup into 4 fruit compotes or dessert dishes. Garnish with a small peach leaf, if desired. Serves 4

PEACHES AND CREAM

3 cups sliced fresh peaches
1 cup sour cream
2 tablespoons sugar
¼ teaspoon grated lemon rind

Place sliced peaches in 6 sherbet glasses. Combine remaining ingredients and spoon over peaches.

Courtesy of Sharon McFall, Busy Woman's Cookbook©

EDEN SPRINGS
HOUSE OF DAVID
BENTON HARBOR
MICH. U.S.A.
SEND FOR LITERATURE
CORRESPONDENCE

POST CARD

STAMP HERE

FOR ADDRESS ONLY

Peach Leather

Farmers going to the field or school children would take it in their lunch for a treat. I learned of this from an historic village in New England.

1/4 pound sugar to 1 pound peaches

Mash peaches as they cook. When dry enough to spread, place in a thin layer on a board greased with butter, set it out in the sun to dry; when dry it can be rolled up like leather. Wrapped up in a cloth, it will keep for a year.

RUM PEACHES

6   *large ripe peaches*
4   *tablespoons sugar*
1   *tablespoon rum*
1   *tablespoon lemon juice*

Peel and slice peaches into a chilled bowl. Combine sugar, rum and lemon juice with peaches. Arrange peaches over a slice of pound cake or serve over vanilla ice cream. Drizzle liquid over peaches.

Thanks to Sallie Carbiener

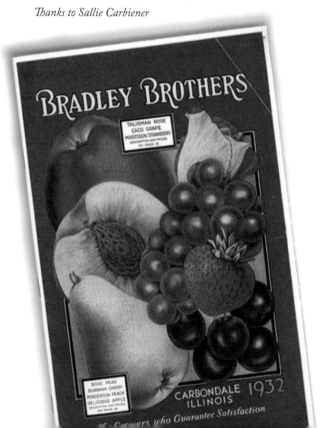

PEACHES AND LACE

6   *fresh ripe firm peaches*
1   *teaspoon lemon juice*
1   *fresh coconut*
¼   *cup confectioner's sugar*
½   *teaspoon almond extract*

Peel, remove stone and slice peaches. Sprinkle lemon juice over the peaches. Coarsely grate the coconut. In a decorative dessert bowl alternate layers of coconut and peaches, making sure each layer is sprinkled with sugar and almond extract. Refrigerate for one hour and serve with pound cake or lady fingers. Serves 8.

SLOW COOKED PEACH APPLESAUCE

10   *Macintosh apples, cored and chopped*
4   *fresh South Carolina peaches, pitted and chopped*
¼   *cups brown sugar*
1   *tablespoon ground cinnamon*
1   *teaspoon pure vanilla extract*

Put fruit into a slow-cooker; sprinkle with sugar and cinnamon. Stir. Turn slow-cooker to high. Cover and cook for 3 hours., then switch to low for 2 hours. Stir in vanilla at end. Serves 12.

Courtesy of South Carolina Peach Council

LEMON PEACH DESSERT

1½ cups sliced fresh peaches
2 tablespoons sugar
2 cups cold milk
1 (4-serving) package instant lemon pudding and pie filling
6 individual sponge cake shells
Whipped topping

Sprinkle peaches with sugar and let stand. Pour milk into a bowl; add pudding mix and beat slowly with hand mixer just until well mixed, about 1minute. Do not over beat. Mixture will be thin. Let stand 5 minutes. Fold in peaches with juice. Spoon into shells. Garnish with whipped topping and additional peach slices.

Thanks to Elaine Jensen, Spring Run Farm, Lowell, Indiana

GARDEN PARTY

6 large firm ripe peaches, peel remove stone, cut in small pieces
¼ cup brown sugar
8 tablespoons butter
2 teaspoons lemon juice
7 basil leaves

Prepare peaches in chilled bowl. Drizzle lemon juice over peach cubes and gently mix. In a heavy medium sauce pan on low heat, melt butter, add sugar, constantly stirring until dissolved then add peaches and gently stir for eight minutes. Tear basil and add to fruit mixture and cook for one more minute. Serve warm in dessert dishes spooned over vanilla ice cream. Garnish with a few red raspberries, if desired. Serves 8.

Jim Shafer instructs Don Minyard in the care of the peaches he has just purchased.

PEACH TRIFLE

1 (3-ounce) package vanilla pudding mix, not instant

1¾ cups low-fat milk

1 (12-ounce) carton frozen whipped topping, thawed

2 tablespoons sugar

5 fresh peaches, peeled and sliced

1 pound cake loaf, cut into 1-inch cubes

½ cup orange juice

Combine pudding mix and milk in saucepan. Bring to a boil over medium heat, stirring constantly until thickened. Remove from heat and cool completely. Fold in half of whipped topping. Sprinkle sugar over peaches; toss gently and set aside. Place half of cake in bottom of trifle bowl and drizzle with half of orange juice. Arrange half of peaches over cake; top with half of pudding mixture. Repeat layers. Spread remaining whipped topping over all. Cover and chill at least 2 hours. Yield: 14 to 16 servings.

Courtesy of Linda Carder Martin, Keep Your Fork Cookbook[©]

GIVE IT A WHIRL!

CARO-WIN

DISTRIBUTED BY
PIEDMONT PEACH GROWERS CO-OP, SPARTANBURG, S.C.

PRODUCE OF U.S.A.

FIGURE FRIENDLY PEACH FRUIT TRIFLE

4 cups fat- free plain yogurt (lemon flavored yogurt works well too)

½ cup Splenda® Granular

2 teaspoons real vanilla extract

9 slices white bread, crusts removed

1 cup sliced strawberries

1 cup fresh raspberries

2 cups peeled, sliced and pitted South Carolina peaches

1 banana, thinly sliced.

6 tablespoons Splenda® Granular

Blend ½ cup of Splenda®, yogurt, and vanilla together in a medium sized mixing bowl. Cut bread into rectangles. Stir together strawberries and 2 tablespoons Splenda®. Gently mix together raspberries with 2 tablespoons Splenda®. Mix together peaches and 2 tablespoons Splenda® Granular. Pour ½ cup of yogurt mixture in the bottom of a large clear glass bowl. Place one-third of the sliced bread on top of the yogurt mixture. Top bread with a third of the peaches, a third of the strawberries and a third of the raspberries. Place a third of the thinly sliced banana on top of the raspberries. Pour a third of the yogurt mixture over the bread and fruit. Repeat steps 2–5 two more times, ending by pouring the remaining yogurt over the fruit. Cover and refrigerate for at least 2 hours or overnight, allowing the bread to fully absorb the fruit juices.

Courtesy of South Carolina Peach Council

PEACH CANAPÉ

2 tablespoons butter
1 tablespoon sugar
2 cups sliced peaches
1 teaspoon lemon juice

Melt butter; peel, stone and slice peaches in butter; cook ten minutes on medium low heat; add sugar and lemon juice, serve on slices of sponge or bunt cake; garnish with cream.

Thanks to Mrs. George J. Ball,
Given by Mrs. Carl (Vivian) Ball

GEORGIA PEACH REFRIGERATOR CAKE

½ pound marshmallows
½ cup orange juice
½ cup ginger ale
1 cup heavy cream, whipped
Sponge cake or lady fingers
6 to 8 fresh Georgia peaches, sliced
½ cup chopped crystallized ginger

Cut marshmallows in quarters, add to orange juice and stir over hot water until almost melted; cool slightly and add ginger ale. When slightly thickened, fold in ¾ cup whipped cream. Line a spring form pan with waxed paper. Arrange layer of cake or ladyfingers on bottom, next a layer of peaches, then layer of marshmallows; repeat until there are 3 layers of cake and 2 of filling. Chill in refrigerator overnight. Unmold; garnish with remaining peaches and cream and ginger.

Courtesy of Dickey Farms, Musella, Georgia, "The Sweetest Peaches in the South"

PEACH TAPIOCA

¼ cup quick-cooking tapioca
1 pint hot water
1 cup sugar
1 tablespoon butter
½ teaspoon salt
1 tablespoon lemon juice
1 cup peach juice
2 cups sliced, canned peaches, reserve juice

Cook the tapioca and water in a double boiler for 15 minutes, add the sugar, butter, salt, lemon juice and peach juice, which has been drained from the peaches. In a greased baking dish, make alternate layers of the tapioca and peaches arranged so that a layer of the peaches comes out on top. Bake in a moderate over (350 degrees) for about 30 minutes, or until brown on top. Serve either hot or cold with cream.

PEACH CRÈME BRULÉE

PEACH BASE:

1   15 oz. can California Cling Peach slices, drained and pureed (about 1 cup)

1   tablespoon sugar

1   teaspoon lemon juice

1   whole egg

CRÈME BRULÉE CUSTARD:

9   large egg yolks

5   tablespoons sugar

2   cups heavy cream

2   teaspoons pure vanilla extract

4½ tablespoons clear sparkling sugar (available at any major grocery store)

Equipment: 8, 5-ounce custard cup molds (disposable aluminum or pyrex). Roasting pan (at least two inches deep and large enough to hold all of the molds). Butane blowtorch.

Preheat oven to 300 degrees. In a one-quart mixing bowl, whisk together the pureed peaches, sugar, lemon juice and egg. Set aside.

In a two-quart mixing bowl, whisk the egg yolks until completely smooth. Pouring the sugar in a steady stream, whisk sugar into egg yolks until yolks are pale yellow. Whisk in the cream and vanilla. This should yield about three cups of custard. Set aside.

Spoon 3 tablespoons of the peach mixture into the bottom of each custard cup molds. Next, gently pour three ounces of the custard mixture over the back of a spoon onto the top of the peach mixture, upsetting the peach mixture as little as possible. This will fill each custard cup mold about ¾ full.

Place the custard cup molds in a roasting pan and fill the pan with hot water half way up the sides of the custard cup molds. Place the uncovered roasting pan in the oven and bake at 300 degrees for one hour or until custard is just set. Do not overcook.

Remove the roasting pan from the oven. Remove the custard cups from the roasting pan and refrigerate until chilled.

To Serve: Remove the custards from the refrigerator. Evenly sprinkle 1½ teaspoons of clear sparkling sugar on top of each the custards.

Light the blowtorch. One custard at a time, carefully and slowly wave the flame about four inches above the sugar until the sugar begins to blister and bubble. Continue until all of the sugar is melted and begins to caramelize. Allow the sugar to cool, about 5 minutes, and serve each crème brûlée with a spoon. Makes: 8 individual crème brûlée cups

Recipe and photo (opposite) courtesy of the California Cling Peach Board and Gary Jenanyan.

C.A. Bingham (opposite upper right) finds the truck a paying proposition. Photo Courtesy Dr. Paul Rood and the State Horticultural Society of Michigan

PEACH PUDDING

1 pint peaches, cover with batter of ½ pint
milk, ½ cup sugar, 1 cup flour, 1 tsp baking powder, 2 eggs, butter the size of a walnut. Bake.

Mrs. Alden Stover

Choice Recipes Compiled by the Ladies Aid of the United Brethren Church, Berrien Springs, Michigan 1924

PEACH BATTER PUDDING

- 2 tablespoons butter
- ¼ cup sugar
- 1 teaspoon salt
- 1 cup flour
- 2 eggs
- 1 cup milk
- 2 cups quartered peaches
- 2 tablespoons lemon juice

Butter a 13 x 9-inch baking dish. Set aside. Mix sugar, salt, flour, eggs, and milk. When smooth, add peaches which have been sprinkled with lemon juice. Pour into buttered baking dish, and bake slowly in a moderate oven (350–375°F) one hour. Serve immediately with wine sauce.

Peach Orchard of R.D. Graham, Grand Rapids, Micigan
Photo Courtesy Dr. Paul Rood and the State Horticultural Society of Michigan

PEACH PUDDING

- 1 cup flour
- 1 cup sugar
- 1 tablespoon baking powder
- 1 cup low fat or regular milk
- 1 stick margarine
- 1 (29-ounce) can peaches
- 1 teaspoon cinnamon
- Juice of 1 lemon

Preheat oven to 325 degrees. Sift flour, sugar and baking powder together; add milk and make batter. Melt margarine in large Pyrex dish. Pour batter over melted margarine. Empty can of peaches, juice and all, over batter. Sprinkle cinnamon and lemon juice on top. Use a knife to carefully swirl mixture. Bake at 325 degrees for 40 minutes.

Thanks to Mavis Lesser

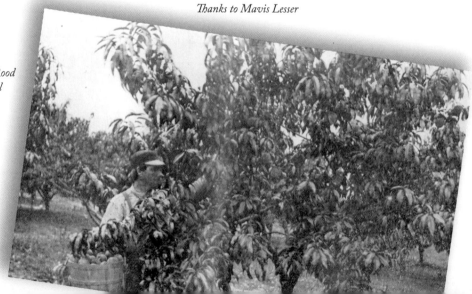

PEACHY RICE PUDDING

Quick to fix: 30 minutes from start to finish

1⅓ cups water

⅔ cup long grained rice

½ of a 12-ounce can evaporated fat free milk

⅓ cup mixed dried fruit bits

2 teaspoons honey

¼ teaspoon pumpkin pie spice or ground cinnamon

⅛ teaspoon salt

1 cup chopped peeled peaches (or frozen sliced peaches, thawed and chopped)

¼ cup vanilla fat free yogurt

In a saucepan, stir together water and uncooked rice. Bring to a boil, reduce heat. Simmer covered for 15–20 minutes, until rice is tender. Stir milk, fruit bits, honey, pumpkin pie spice or cinnamon and salt together. Bring to a boil. Reduce heat. Simmer uncovered over medium heat about 5 minutes or until thick and creamy. Stir frequently. Serve warm with peaches and yogurt. Serves 4.

Thanks to Bettye J. Knott, Waxahachie, Texas

OATMEAL PEACH PUDDING

2 cups canned peaches, fresh rhubarb or apples

2 tablespoons lemon juice

¼ teaspoon cinnamon

1 tablespoon butter

¼ cup solid vegetable shortening, melted

⅓ cup packed brown sugar

⅔ cup sifted flour

⅛ teaspoon salt

¼ teaspoon baking soda

⅔ cup quick cooking oats

½ teaspoon vanilla extract

Preheat oven to 350 degrees. Arrange fruit in shallow, greased baking dish. Sprinkle fruit with lemon juice and cinnamon, and dot with butter. In a separate bowl, combine melted shortening and brown sugar. Set aside. In a large bowl, sift flour, salt, and soda together. Add oatmeal. Blend in brown sugar mixture, crumbling well. Add vanilla extract. Mix lightly and spread over fruit. Bake in preheated oven for 45 minutes. Serve warm with pudding sauce.

PEACH ICE CREAM

1 quart milk plus 1 cup (or more depending
   on amount of fruit to be used)
1 can sweetened condensed milk
1 small can evaporated milk
1 pint whipping cream
1 cup sugar
3 tablespoons vanilla flavoring
3 cups (or less) mashed peaches (fresh),
   mixed with ¾ cups sugar and juice of
   1 lemon.

Combine first 6 ingredients and freeze to a mush in an electric or hand-turned freezer. Add peach mixture and freeze hard. Remove dasher and pack with ice and salt until ready to serve. Keeps well in deep freeze without getting icy.

GEORGIA PEACH ICE CREAM #1

1 quart plus 1 cup milk
1 (14-ounce) can sweetened condensed milk
1 (6-ounce) can evaporated milk
1 pint whipping cream
3 tablespoons vanilla
1¾ cups sugar, divided
3 cups mashed fresh Georgia peaches
Juice of 1 lemon

In the can of an ice cream freezer, combine the first five ingredients and 1 cup of the sugar and mix well. Freeze according to manufacturer's directions until mixture forms a "mush." In a bowl, combine mashed peaches, remaining sugar and lemon juice and mix well. Combine with milk mixture and freeze until hard.

Courtesy of Dickey Farms, Musella, Georgia, "The Sweetest Peaches in the South"

GEORGIA PEACH ICE CREAM #2

3 cups peach pulp
1 tablespoon lemon juice
2 cups sugar, divided
¼ teaspoon salt
4 eggs, slightly beaten
2 quarts milk
1 pint whipping cream
¼ teaspoon almond flavoring
Ice and ice cream salt

To the peach pulp add the lemon juice and 1 cup of the sugar, let stand 1 hour. Add the other cup of sugar and salt to the beaten eggs and blend in half of the milk. Cook this sugar, egg, and milk mixture over boiling water to make a thick custard. Cool. Add the remainder of milk, the cream that has been partially whipped, the flavoring, and sweetened peach pulp. Freeze using 1 part salt to 6 parts ice. Yield: 1 gallon.

Courtesy of Dickey Farms, Musella, Georgia, "The Sweetest Peaches in the South"

GEORGIA PEACH ICE CREAM #3

2½ pounds fresh Georgia peaches, chopped
½ cup white sugar
1 pint half-and-half cream
1 (14-ounce) can sweetened condensed milk
1 (12-ounce) can evaporated milk
1 teaspoon vanilla extract
2 cups whole milk, or as needed

Puree peaches with the sugar and half-and-half in batches in a blender or food processor. In a gallon ice cream freezer container, mix together the peach mixture, sweetened condensed milk, evaporated milk, and vanilla. Pour in enough whole milk to fill the container to the fill line, about 2 cups. Follow the manufacturer's instructions to freeze the ice cream. Yield: 32 servings.

Tip: You can make this ice cream a little sweeter by adding up to ½ cup more sugar.

Courtesy of Dickey Farms, Musella, Georgia, "The Sweetest Peaches in the South"

TEXAN'S PEACH ICE CREAM

Said to be President Lyndon B. Johnson's favorite!

1 quart cream
1 pint milk
3 eggs
1 cup sugar
½ gallon soft peaches, mashed and well sweetened

Make a boiled custard of cream, milk, eggs, and sugar. When cooled, add sweetened peaches. Freeze. This makes 1 gallon of delicious ice cream.

Thanks to Mrs. Lillian Knight, Published by www.gotfruit.com

PEACH ICE CREAM

8 large eggs
3 cups sugar
1 cup Eagle Brand® condensed milk
2 quarts half and half
1 cup Milnot or Carnation evaporated milk
1 quart whipping cream
2 teaspoons vanilla extract
2 large ripe peaches, peeled, stoned, mashed

Beat eggs with mixer until frothy. Add sugar and beat again. Add Eagle Brand Milk, half and half, Carnation milk and whipping cream. Mix thoroughly. Add vanilla and peaches. Mix again and pour into a 1½-gallon old fashioned church ice cream freezer. If freezer compartment is not full, top off with whole milk.

Best if made early in the morning and put into a deep freezer until time to serve.

Thanks to Aunt Sis McFadden

PEACH ICE SHERBET

1 envelope unflavored gelatin
3 cups whole milk, divided
2 cups regular half and half
2 cups sugar
2 cups peach nectar
2 drops yellow food coloring
1 drop red food coloring
¾ teaspoon salt
2 cups coarsely chopped Georgia peaches
¼ teaspoon vanilla extract

In a saucepan, combine gelatin and 1 cup of the milk. Heat until gelatin dissolves.

In a large bowl, combine remaining ingredients and add gelatin mixture last. Pour mixture into 4-quart can for the ice cream freezer. Churn sherbet according to manufacturers directions. Once sherbet has finished churning, allow to ripen for 2–3 hours. Yield: 15 servings.

Note: This recipe was tested with an electric ice cream maker. The churning time is 35 minutes; other ice cream machines may vary.

Courtesy of Georgia Department of Agriculture

FRESH PEACH RASPBERRY SHERBET

⅓ cup sugar
⅓ cup condensed milk
¾ cup undiluted frozen orange juice
6 medium, ripe peaches peeled, pitted and cut in wedges
½ pint red raspberries

Place in blender and blend until it reaches a smooth consistency. Pour into a container to freeze. Serve in fruit compotes with a few fresh red raspberries on top. Serves 6–8.

Thomas Jefferson is one of our most revered statesmen and one of our greatest horticulturists. His favorite fruit was the peach and he raised 37 varieties. Detail of portrait by Charles Wilson Peale, 1791.

SWEET AND TANGY SUMMER SORBET

4 medium fresh peaches and/or nectarines
1 cup water
2 cups sugar
½ cup lemon liqueur (limoncello)
2 tablespoons lemon juice
Extra peach and/or nectarine slices (optional garnish)

Peel, pit, and puree fruit until smooth in a blender or food processor; set aside and chill. Stir together water and sugar in a medium saucepan and bring to a boil. Reduce heat and simmer for 2 to 3 minutes or until sugar is dissolved. Refrigerate until well chilled; stir in fruit puree, liqueur and lemon juice. Transfer to the bowl of an ice cream maker and freeze according to manufacturer's instructions. Cover and freeze for at least 1 hour or up to 3 days. Spoon into small dishes and garnish with fresh fruit slices and mint, if desired.

Courtesy of California Cling Peach Board

GEORGIA PEACH SORBET

3 cups water
1 cup sugar
3 cups chopped fresh Georgia peaches
¾ cup fresh orange juice
¼ cup lemon juice
¼ teaspoon almond extract

Bring water and sugar to a boil in a medium saucepan, stirring often; reduce heat, and simmer 5 minutes, stirring occasionally. Cool; cover and chill. Process peach slices and lemon juice in a blender or food processor until smooth, stopping once to scrape down sides. Combine sugar mixture, peach mixture, orange juice, and almond extract; pour into freezer container of a 4-quart hand-turned or electric freezer. Freeze according to manufacturer's instructions. Pack freezer with additional ice and rock salt, and let stand 1 hour before serving. Yield: 7 cups

Courtesy of Dickey Farms, Musella, Georgia, "The Sweetest Peaches in the South"

```
PEACH ICE

1½ cups sugar
1 quart canned peaches, including liquid
Juice and pulp of one orange
Juice and pulp of two lemons
Water to make 2 quarts

Combine all ingredients, the sugar being well dissolved.
Freeze. When nearly done, add 1 egg white beaten. This
makes 2 quarts.

Original contributor: Mrs. Fred Renfro, Cottage Bend Club

From a 1933 Fannin County Texas Home Demonstration Clubs'
Cookbook
```

RAINBOW POPS

1½ cups fresh or frozen blackberries, thawed
1 tablespoon sugar or Splenda®
1 cup peeled sliced South Carolina peaches
Dash lemon juice
1½ cups cubed honeydew melon
Dash of salt

Place berries and sugar in blender, process till smooth. Strain mixture through a fine mesh sieve into a bowl; discard solids. Set aside. Puree peaches and juice in blender; set aside. Puree melon and salt; set aside. Spoon 2 tablespoons blackberry mixture into 6 (3-ounce) ice-pop molds. Top with 2 tablespoons peach puree. Spoon 2 tablespoons melon puree over peach layer. Place sticks in center of molds. Freeze 6 hours or until frozen.

Courtesy of South Carolina Peach Council

BLOB DESSERT

1 cup Cool Whip® Free
1 large box (or 2 small) Sugar Free Peach Jell-O®
1 (12-ounce) can of diet cream soda

Completely dissolve Jell-O® into 2 cups boiling water. Add soda. Refrigerate until "wiggly" (about 2 hours, but no longer). Use an electric mixer to stir in Cool Whip® until completely mixed. Return to fridge until very firm (overnight is best). Serves 4.

Courtesy of South Carolina Peach Council

Buyer Jerry Boynbon, Ft. Wayne, Indiana picks up 2 bushels of 3-inch Golden Jubilie. The grower, Fred Faher, right, has been bringing fruit for fifteen years. August 1939.

Uncle Henry Bartz with his truck being loaded with peaches for delivery.

In the sorting room. Cousin Edwin Bartz, sixth from left, Aunt Adelia, seated, and Uncle Henry, standing in back.

PEACH AND MELON DESSERT

2 tablespoons fresh orange juice
2 tablespoons peach liqueur
2 tablespoons honey
4 large ripe peaches
2 cups diced cantaloupe
2 cups diced honeydew melon

Mix the orange juice, peach liqueur and honey in a small bowl and set aside. Slice peaches into wedges and gently combine with melons. Pour syrup over fruit and mix gently. Refrigerate one hour. Serve cold as a delicious natural non-fat dessert or use as a topping for yogurt or ice cream.

PEACH WITH HONEY SYRUP

4 ripe peaches
½ cup honey
4-quart saucepan
Enough cold water to cover peaches
Chocolate bar (your favorite)
Ice cubes

Using a sharp knife, lightly score bottom (not stem end) of each peach with hatch marks.

Prepare ice bath and set aside. Place peaches in a large (4-quart) saucepan and fill with enough cold water to cover peaches. Remove peaches. Over high heat, bring water to a boil and blanch peaches in boiling water. Boil for 1 minute (more if skin is not pulling away from peach.) Use a slotted spoon and immediately transfer peaches to ice bath. Remove peaches from ice water and peel. Set peaches and skins aside.

Reserve 4 cups of poaching liquid in pan, add skins and honey. Bring to a boil and cook until reduced to 1½ cups. Pour liquid through a sieve, set over a bowl, and discard skins. Immediately spoon syrup over peaches, and serve with your favorite chocolate bar.

Janet Snyder, Glad Peach Bake Fest Winner, Coloma, Michigan

Jams, Jellies, & Preserves

PRESERVED PEACHES

4 *pounds peaches*
4 *pounds sugar*
4 *cups water*

Pare, cut in halves, and take out stones. Arrange peaches and sugar in layers in pre-serving kettle; let stand over night. In morning simmer until peaches are tender; fill jars with fruit, boil syrup five minutes, fill jars with syrup, and seal.

OPEN KETTLE PEACHES

Select firm, ripe peaches. Peel or dip peaches in hot water, then in cold and slip off peel. Leave whole or cut in halves or slices. Boil 20 minutes in No. 2 or No. 3 syrup. Pack in clean, hot, sterilized jars. Seal tightly.

PICKLED PEACHES

Remove the down from the skins by rubbing with a coarse towel, and stick three cloves into each peach. To 7 pounds of fine peaches, use one quart of best vinegar and four pounds of sugar. Cook the sugar and vinegar together to a syrup, skim well as it boils, put in the peaches and let them simmer until tender enough to easily be pierced with a straw. Take out and put in a jar. Pour over the boiling hot syrup and seal at once. Hard yellow peaches are best for this recipe.

From: Vegetarian Cook Book, Eden Springs, Israelite House of David, 1912

PICKLED PEACHES

10 *pounds peaches*
3 *pounds light brown sugar*
1 *quart vinegar*
1 *ounce cinnamon*
1 *ounce ground cloves*

Boil peaches until tender. Boil syrup ½ hour longer. Put in jars and seal.

Choice Recipes Compiled by the Ladies Aid of the United Brethren Church, Berrien Springs, Michigan 1924

PICKLED PEACHES

Select firm, ripe peaches. Peel and put into jar closely. Use sweet spiced vinegar, tie whole spices in cheesecloth. Bring vinegar to boil, pour over the peaches. Repeat each day for nine days. Keep peaches submerged under the vinegar. Six cloves stuck into peaches in random patterns will make them look nice. Do not have to seal.

TO PEEL AND PREPARE PEACHES FOR PICKLES

> 2 tablespoons red lye
> 1 gallon boiling hot water

Put lye into the water. Keep at boiling point. Dip six peaches in at a time for one minute, remove and drop into a pan of cold water. Rub off the peeling with a coarse cloth. Change the cold water occasionally if many are fixed, and use fresh water. Rinse the cloth as it takes a rough cloth to remove peelings. A wire strainer makes a good receptacle with which to dip peaches.

SILVER MOUNTAIN VINEGAR

Jack Silver has been a chef to the stars, including Sir Elton John. He has worked as a chef at the renowned Four Seasons Hotel in Austin, Texas and now owns his own business – Silver Mountain Vinegar.

His bottles are truly a culinary art form. His customers say, "It's too pretty to open!" He points out that his vinegar bottles do not need refrigeration, so the customer can display the bottle in the kitchen until it is used.

Jack is a creative chef as well as a funny stand up comic. I am fortunate to call him a good friend. I asked him to prepare a peach white house recipe. This was his answer and I have to say they are a special treat with a casual or informal dinner.

GUEST WORKER PEACHES

Simply half 3 peaches and fill vacant seed cavity with ½ teaspoon brown sugar, and ½ teaspoon butter. Sprinkle with cinnamon and broil for 5 minutes and serve over ice cream.

PICKLED GEORGIA PEACHES

- ½ teaspoon Fruit Fresh®
- 2 quarts cold water
- 8 pounds fresh Georgia peaches, peeled
- 6¾ cups sugar
- 1 quart vinegar
- 2 tablespoons whole cloves, crushed
- 1 tablespoon coarsely chopped gingerroot
- 4 (2-inch) cinnamon sticks

In a large bowl, combine Fruit Fresh® and water; add peaches. In a saucepan, combine sugar and vinegar; stir to dissolve sugar and heat to boiling. Boil for 5 minutes; skimming foam. Place cloves, gingerroot and cinnamon in a cheesecloth spice bag and place in syrup. Drain peaches and place in boiling syrup. Cook until tender but not soft. Cool and refrigerate overnight. Bring syrup and peaches to a boil; remove spice bag. Pack peaches into hot, sterilized jars; cover with syrup, leaving ½-inch headspace. Process according to jar manufacturer's specifications. Yield: 6 (half-pint) jars.

Courtesy of Dickey Farms, Musella, Georgia, "The Sweetest Peaches in the South"

SWEET PEACH PICKLE

- 1 peck ripe firm peaches
- 7 pounds sugar
- 1 pint vinegar
- 1 quart water
- 2 dozen whole cloves
- 3 tablespoons broken stick cinnamon

Prepare peaches, pealing with a rough cloth. Boil sugar, vinegar and water into a moderate thick syrup. Add spices tied in cheesecloth. Add peaches, boil until they can be stuck with straw to the pit. Stir occasionally for even cooking. Fill jars with peaches. Continue boiling syrup until heavy, then add to peaches, covering well. Add one small cinnamon scented geranium leaf to top. Seal.

SWEET PICKLED PEACHES

Place peaches into a large bowl and cover with boiling water. Let stand for one minute. Remove from water and wipe dry. Remove skin with a sharp knife. Insert 3 or 4 whole cloves into each peach. Place peaches in jars or a large crock and cover with hot vinegar, allowing 3 ½ cups corn syrup for each quart of vinegar used. Every morning for a week, pour off the vinegar, heat to boiling and pour over peaches again. On the last day, seal jars or cover crock well.

Augusta Gast Totzke

SPICED PEACHES

The Ball family were the founders of what is now the largest quality seed and horticultural products company in the world, Ball Horticultural Company.

1 cup vinegar
3 pounds brown sugar
4 pounds peaches
1 tablespoon cinnamon
1 tablespoon clove
1 teaspoon ginger
1 teaspoon salt
⅛ teaspoon cayenne pepper

Boil vinegar and sugar. Scald peaches, remove skins, and cook in syrup. Tie spices in bag and cook with peaches. When peaches are tender, pour into stone jars, reheat syrup every day for a week, pouring over peaches when boiling. All kinds of small fruits may be spiced in this manner.

Mrs. George J. Ball, Given by Mrs. Carl "Vivian" Ball

This picture was taken on Carl Ball's 50th birthday. He kept it on his desk until he passed away in 2004. His daughter, Anna Caroline, the current CEO of Ball Horticultural Co. gave the framed picture to me. It is with love and respect I have presented it here.

BRANDIED PEACHES

4 pounds peaches
2 cups water
4 pounds sugar
2 cups brandy

Cut peaches into halves, remove stones, and cook in sugar and water syrup five minutes; take out, remove skins, and cook again in syrup five minutes. Remove kettle from range, and let peaches stand in syrup over night. In morning reheat, pack peaches in jars, and fill jars with an equal quantity of syrup and brandy. Seal.

OLD FASHIONED SPICED PEACHES

1½ pints sugar
2 pints water
1 cupful vinegar
1 tablespoonful whole cloves
2 tablespoonfuls broken cinnamon bark

Pare, halve, and remove stones from large, cling stone peaches. Place the sugar, water and vinegar in a kettle with the spices tied in a muslin bag; let boil five minutes, then drop in the fruit and continue boiling until tender. Take the peaches out carefully with a silver fork and pack them in jars. Fill jars with the syrup and seal. A few cracked peach stones boiled in the syrup improve the flavor.
From: Vegetarian Cook Book, Eden Springs, Israelite House of David, 1912

PEACH BUTTER

- 1 peck peaches
- 2 quarts cider, boiled
- 2 tablespoons lemon juice
- ¼ cup granulated sugar

Pare and cut peaches into small pieces; add cider and lemon juice, boil until thick, stirring constantly; add sugar. Fill jars and seal.

PEACH BUTTER - SUGAR FREE

- 2 quarts very ripe peaches, peeled, pitted and chopped
- 3 cups apple cider
- 1 cup white grape juice (concentrated-sim-mered down from 2 cups)
- 2 tablespoons lemon juice
- ¼ to ½ teaspoon almond extract (optional)

Place all ingredients (except almond extract) in large non-aluminum kettle. Cook over low heat until thick, stirring frequently and skimming if necessary. When butter reaches suitable thickness, taste and add extract if desired. Pour into sterile half pint or pint jars, cap with sterile lids. Place jars in boiling water, let water return to boiling temperature and process 15 minutes. Makes 6–7 cups.

SPICED PEACH BUTTER

- ¾ cup unsalted butter, softened
- 1 fully ripe, firm peach, remove pit, cube but do not peel
- 2 tablespoons honey
- ¾ teaspoon fresh lemon juice
- ½ teaspoon grated lemon zest
- ½ teaspoon ground cinnamon
- ¼ teaspoon freshly grated nutmeg

Cream butter in a food processor. Add peach cubes a few at a time through the food tube, processing until smooth. Add remaining ingredients and blend well. Pack the spiced peach butter into a crock. Cover and refrigerate.

Author's Note: A log can be made by rolling the butter and then covering it with plastic wrap. Refrigerate or keep it in the freezer for up to 2 months.

Lee Totzke

STRATFORD LITTLE JELLY FACTORY

What began as a cherished hobby for a beautiful stay at home mom has turned into a thriving business

In 1998 Amanda Savage decided to buy peaches from Stratford, Oklahoma growers and she wanted to pick her own. She packaged them and off she would go to set up at the Ada Farmer's Market. Sometimes she wouldn't sell all of her peaches. To keep them from spoiling she would get out her kettles and canning supplies, making peach jellies like her grandmother taught her as a little girl.

When her pantry was full, she decided she needed to do something with all the jelly, so she started selling the famous Oklahoma Statford peaches in jars.

Her Sur Jel box said "never double the recipe", so for the first two years she made her jelly seven pints at a time. You can only smile at the naivety of this young entrepreneur. Another eye opener was when someone told her she couldn't be making jelly in her kitchen and selling it. Amanda's reaction was "Really?"

Few can pass by her Stratford Little Jelly Factory without stopping to browse and buy. She now produces 60 gallons of various jellies at a time. You can enjoy her cobbler recipe on page 158.

PEACH JAM

1 orange, rind and all
8 cups sliced ripe peaches
2 tablespoons lemon juice
8 cups sugar
1 cup crushed pineapple
¾ cup maraschino cherries
Lemon geranium leaves

Grind orange in a food processor. Set aside. Slice peaches in half. Immediately pour lemon juice over peaches. Add sugar and ground orange rind. Let stand overnight. In the morning, place in a large saucepan. Add pineapple to peach mixture. Boil for 20 minutes or until thick. Add cherries and boil an additional 2 minutes. Pour hot mixture into prepared jars. Place lemon geranium leaf on top and seal.

PEACH JAM

2⅛ cups prepared fruit*
3¾ cups sugar
½ bottle fruit pectin

*To prepare the fruit: peel and pit about 1½ pounds fully ripe peaches. Crush or chop very fine. Measure 2⅛ cups into a large sauce pan. (If the peaches lack tartness, use only 2 cups fruit and add 2 tablespoons lemon juice.)

To make the jam: Add sugar to fruit in saucepan and mix well. Cook over high heat, bring to a full rolling boil, and boil hard for one minute. Stir constantly.

Remove from heat and stir in bottled fruit pectin. Stir and skim by turns for 3 minutes to cool slightly and to prevent floating fruit. Pour quickly into glasses. Paraffin at once. Makes about 6 six-ounce glasses.

MICROWAVE PEACH REFRIGERATOR JAM

2 cups fresh peaches, peeled, pitted and mashed

4 cups sugar

2 tablespoons lemon juice

2 teaspoons ascorbic-citric powder (Fresh Fruit®)

¼ teaspoon ground cinnamon

1 (3-ounce) package liquid pectin (Sure Gel®)

Combine first 5 ingredients in a 5-quart casserole. Microwave, uncovered at HIGH for 5 minutes, stir well. Microwave, uncovered, at HIGH for 15–17 minutes, or until mixture reaches a full rolling boil. Stir in pectin, skim off foam with spoon. Pour into hot sterilized jars, leaving ¼-inch headspace. Cover with metal lids, and screw on bands. Let stand at room temperature until cool. Store in refrigerator up to 3 weeks. Yield: 7 half-pints.

Courtesy of Texas Hill Country Fruit Council

CANTALOUPE AND PEACH PRESERVES

2 pounds South Carolina peaches

2 pounds cantaloupe

¼ teaspoon salt

4 lbs. or 8 cups sugar

½ teaspoon cinnamon

Peel and slice peaches. Peel, seed and slice cantaloupe in small pieces. Combine peaches, cantaloupe, and sugar. Stir until sugar is dissolved. Bring to boil. Add cinnamon and salt. Cook until thick stirring occasionally. Pour in sterilized jars and seal. Yield: 5 pints.

Courtesy of South Carolina Peach Council

night, then cook until tender and put through coarse grinder. Then add sugar and pineapple, and cook until thick.

PEACH MARMALADE

1 pound peaches   ¾ pound sugar

Peel peaches, cut in halves, and take out stones. Crack a few of the stones, take out the kernels, pour boiling water over them and rub off the skins; then cut lengthwise in small strips. Weigh the peaches, add sugar and cook slowly on the back of the stove; when it boils, stir constantly and continue to boil until thick. Add the kernels five minutes before removing from stove. Put in jars and seal.

From: Vegetarian Cook Book, Israelite House of David, as reorganized by Mary Purnell, 1934

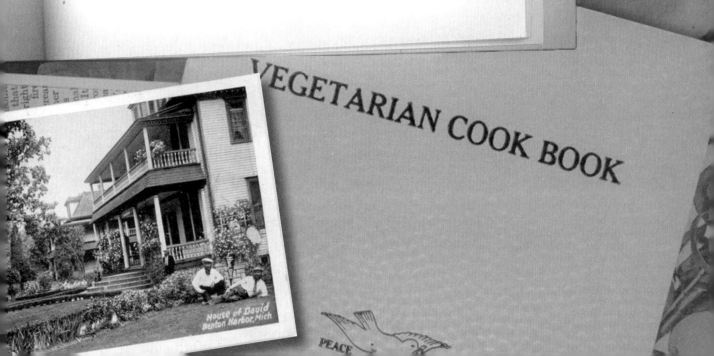

GEORGIA PEACH CHUTNEY

1 tablespoon cooking oil
½ cup chopped onion
1 to 2 teaspoons grated gingerroot
2 cloves garlic, minced
⅓ cup sugar
2 teaspoons cornstarch
¼ cup balsamic vinegar or red wine vinegar
1 tablespoon lemon juice
¼ teaspoon dry mustard
¼ teaspoon ground allspice
Dash ground cloves
1½ cups chopped, peeled Georgia peaches
½ cup dried tart red cherries or raisins
⅓ cup toasted chopped almonds (optional)

Heat cooking oil in a medium saucepan. Cook onion, gingerroot, and garlic in hot oil until tender but not brown. Stir together the sugar and cornstarch. Stir into saucepan. Stir in vinegar, lemon juice, mustard, allspice, and cloves until well blended. Stir in the peaches and cherries or raisins. Cook and stir until slightly thickened and heated through. If desired, stir in almonds. Serve warm as an accompaniment to ham. Yield: about 2 cups.

Courtesy of Dickey Farms, Musella, Georgia, "The Sweetest Peaches in the South"

Christian Nitz won several championships at Michigans largest youth fair, one was for his peach preserves.

ROSY PEACH CHUTNEY

15 tomatoes, peeled and chopped

5 fresh South Carolina peaches, peeled, pitted and chopped

5 red apples, peeled, cored and diced

4 medium onions, diced

4 stalks celery, diced

1½ cups distilled white vinegar

1 tablespoon salt

1 cup pickling spice, wrapped in cheesecloth

Combine tomatoes, peaches, apples, onions, celery, vinegar, salt and pickling spice in a large stockpot. Bring to a boil, then reduce heat to low, and simmer for about 2 hours, or until thickened. Transfer to sterile jars and store in the refrigerator, or freeze in plastic containers.

Courtesy of South Carolina Peach Council

PEACH CHUTNEY

Good served with chicken and pork dinners.

10 pounds firm ripe peaches

1 pound seedless raisins

1 pound dates, chopped

½ pound dried cherries, chopped

4 cups vinegar

½ cup lime juice

2 lemons

5 cups sugar

1 cup candied ginger, coarsely chopped

1 cup nuts, chopped

Pare and cut peaches in small pieces. Add raisins, dates, cherries, vinegar and juice. Quarter lemons; remove seeds and slice very thin. Add to fruit mixture. Cook until peaches are soft, stirring constantly. Add sugar. When mixture is thick, add ginger and nuts. Sterilize jars; pack and seal. Makes 14 half-pints.

PEACH GLAZE FOR BBQ RIBS

- 1 cup slightly ripe Georgia peaches, pureed well
- 2 tablespoons peach nectar
- 2 tablespoons sugar
- 1 tablespoon soy sauce
- 1½ teaspoons corn starch
- 1 teaspoon minced garlic
- ½ teaspoon powdered ginger

Combine all ingredients in a large saucepan. Bring to boil, reduce heat and simmer for 6–8 minutes. Apply glaze with brush, to evenly coat meat. Grill as desired.

Courtesy of Georgia Department of Agriculture

GEORGIA PEACH RIB SAUCE

- 1 (6 ounce) jar peach baby food
- 2 tablespoons soy sauce
- ½ cup firmly packed brown sugar
- 2 garlic cloves, minced*
- ⅓ cup ketchup
- 1 teaspoon ground ginger
- ⅓ cup white vinegar

Stir together all ingredients; place in an airtight 2-cup jar, and chill up to 2 weeks. Use as a grilling or basting sauce for pork chops, ribs, or chicken. Yield: 1½ cups.

* 1 tablespoon garlic powder may be substituted.

Courtesy of Dickey Farms, Musella, Georgia, "The Sweetest Peaches in the South"

CALIFORNIA CLING PEACH COUNTRY BARBECUE SAUCE

Also serve as condiment for grilled chicken, beef or pork.

- 1 (16-ounce) can California cling peaches in juice or extra light syrup
- ¾ cup ketchup
- ⅓ cup honey
- 3 tablespoons prepared mustard
- 2 tablespoons cider vinegar
- 1 tablespoon grated fresh ginger
- 1 large clove garlic, minced

Drain peaches, reserving all liquid. Combine reserved peach liquid with ketchup, honey, prepared mustard, vinegar, ginger and garlic. Bring to a boil in a small saucepan. Boil 5 minutes, stirring frequently. Serve as desired.

For delicious country ribs, place ribs (3 pounds pork spareribs) on a charcoal grill about 6 inches from heat source. Cover and cook slowly, about 1 hour, turning occasionally. Brush ribs with sauce during the last 20 minutes of grilling. Serve with grilled vegetable skewers. Makes: 5–6 servings.

Recipe and photo courtesy of the California Cling Peach Board

PEACH BASIL MAYONNAISE

This is good with grilled chicken, fish or veggies, and steamed broccoli, cauliflower or asparagus.

   1 South Carolina peach, diced
   ¼ cup egg substitute
Zest of ½ lime (1 teaspoon)
Juice of 2 limes (¼ cup)
   2 cloves garlic, cut in half
Small handful of basil leaves (½ cup)
   ¼ teaspoon black pepper
   ¼ teaspoon salt
   ¾ cup olive oil

Process peaches, egg substitute, zest and juice, garlic, basil, pepper and salt in a food processor or blender until smooth. Scrape down sides of container to ensure a smooth mixture. With the cover on and the processor running, gradually add the olive oil in a thin stream through the top passageway and process until mayonnaise is smooth and creamy. Serve at room temperature or chill up to 2 weeks. Makes 1⅓ cups

Courtesy of South Carolina Peach Council

Martha's

Take an influential, hardworking couple with three grown children with families and active careers, one husband who owns one of the busiest Chevrolet dealerships in Texas, one very active, energetic wife, mother and grandmother and you have a small glimpse of the Lewis family. They are well-known in East Texas for their ownership of a large portion of the world famous First Monday Trade Days grounds and pavilions in Canton Texas. Their business attracts millions of visitors every year and "First Monday" is one of the oldest Trade Days in the country. Martha Lewis found the time to own her own restaurant, small and picturesque with a tree growing through the center of the roof. She recently established a new restaurant that is four times the size of the old one (what was she thinking?) and still lives in the same home she and her husband have shared for their entire married life. Martha Lewis is just like the rest of us. That is, if the rest of us happen to be talented, loving, creative cooks and bakers, and unbelievably energetic. I am always struck by her devotion to her family and friends and her complete lack of pretension.

We operate one of the largest home décor and seasonal merchandise spaces in the Original Pavilion, adjacent to her restaurant, Martha's. We share many of the same customers and they all rave about her plethora of pies—especially Martha's Texas peach pie.

The recipes she shares in this book are from her private collection, served only to family and friends.

Thank you, Martha!

● You can visit her family's business on the web: *www.cantontradedays.com*

REFERENCES AND COOKBOOKS

100ᵗʰ Anniversary Cookbook, Zion United Church of Christ, Baroda, Michigan.

Baptist Church Cookbook, Chappell Hill, Texas, 1927.

Busy Woman's Cookbook, Creative Ideas Publishing, Tallahassee, Florida, 2001.

Cookbook, Fannin County Home Demonstration Clubs, Texas, 1933.

Eating Good, Texas/New Mexico, Power Company.

Family Recipes, First Presbyterian Church, Hammond, Indiana.

First Report of the Secretary of Agriculture, J.M. Rush, First Secretary of Agriculture, 1889.

Keep Your Fork Cookbook, Linda Carder Martin, Athens, Texas, 2004.

Leisure Hour Library, Modern Cook Book and Medical Guide, 1889.

Old Fashioned Gardening, Grace Tabor, 1913.

Our Family Cookbook, Gaston Episcopal Hospital, Dallas, Texas

Peaches of New York, V.P. Hedrick, 1916.

Taste of Tradition, St. John's Lutheran Church, Baroda, Michigan.

Vegetarian Cookbook, Mary's City of David, Benton Harbor, Michigan, 1912 and 1933.

War Garden Victorious, Charles Lathrop Pack, 1919.

CONTRIBUTORS

Carol and Randy Arnold (www.4thischild.com)

Don Baiers, President of Michigan Peach Sponsor Board, Baiers Orchards, 7980 Territorial Road, Watervliet, Michigan 49098, 269-463-3351 (funnyfarm@qtm.net)

Dr. Liberty Hyde Bailey Museum, 903 S. Bailey Avenue, South Haven, Michigan, and Bailey Hortorium

Dick Bartz

Karl Bayer, Tri City Record, Watervliet, Michigan

Kathy Bejma, KD Vintage, (www.kdvintage.com)

California Cling Peach Board

Sallie and Terry Carbiener

Cash Farms, 2008 Battleground Road, Cowpens, South Carolina, 29330 (www.cashfarmsinc.com)

Cornell University, Ithaca, New York

Ed Czuba, 6910 Angling Road, Coloma, Michigan 49038

Dickey Farms, "The Sweetest Peaches in the South", 3440 Old Hwy 341, Musella, Georgia, 1-800-732-2442 (www.gapeaches.com/index.htm)

Jimmy Duecker, Burgs Corner Fruit Stand, Stonewall, Texas 78671, 830-644-2401

Mrs. Mona Duer, Hooker, Oklahoma

Echo Communications Staff, Emeryville, California, 510-654-5400

Mrs. Paul Fast, Hooker, Oklahoma

Barbara Ferris

Paul Friday's Flamin' Fury Peaches, Grower and Breeder, 2155 Friday Road, Coloma, Michigan 49038 (www.flaminfury.com)

Fruit Acres Farm, Randy and Annette Friday Bjorge, 2559 Friday Road, Coloma, Michigan 49038 (www.fruitacresfarms.com)

Georgia Peach Commission and Staff

Polly Godrey, Eva, Oklahoma

Gotfruit, Ukiah, California, 800-455-7020 (www.gotfruit.com)

Don and Kathy Gross, Austin Woodhenge (www.austinwoodhenge.com)

Archie Haynes

The Herald-Palladium, Michael Eliasohn and William F. Ast III, 3450 Hollywood Road, St. Joseph, Michigan, 49085

Saundra Horblitt

Elaine Jensen, Spring Run Farm, Folk Art and Antiques, Lowell, Indiana 46356

Bettye J. Knott, Waxahachie, Texas

Lane Packing Company, Highway 96 East and 50 Lane Road, Fort Valley, Georgia, 31030, 800-277-3224 (www.lanepacking.com/contactus.da)

Rick and Sophie Lausman

Margaret Leatz

Martha Lewis, Canton, Texas (www.cantontradedays.com)

Lincoln's New Salem Historic Site, Petersburg, Illinois 62675, 275-632-3443

Gary Marberger Orchards, Fredericksburg, Texas 78624, 830-997-9433

Brooksie Malone, Waxahachie, Texas

Linda Martin, Athens, Texas, Keep Your Fork Cookbook

Sis McFadden

Sharon and Gene McFall, Creative Ideas Publishing (www.busy-womanscookbook.com)

Janice Mensinger

Dannie, Jerita, Jo and Lora Minyard, Marietta, Oklahoma

Rebekah Mize

Mike Muirhead

Robert C. Myers, Berrien County Historical Association, Berrien Springs, Michigan 49103 (www.berrienhistory.org)

National Peach Council, Charles Walker, Director

Sherri and Todd Nitz

Vic Nixon

Parkland Books, Marge and Ed Rothfuss, Used and Rare Book Dealers, 850 Lake Blaine Road, Kalispell, Montana 59901, 406-752-4464

Dave and Doris Pesko

Kenneth R. Pott, Executive Director, Fort Miami Heritage Society, Priscilla V. Byrns Heritage Center, 708 Market St., St. Jospeh, Michigan 49085 (www.fortmiami.org)

Virginia Radewald

Nancy Rains

Dr. Paul J. Rood, 72723 CR 378, Covert, Michigan 49043

Joe Sage Peach and Blueberry Farm, 3401 Duncan Road, Hagar Township, Michigan, 49022, 269-925-1019

Luis Sandoval, Nye Farms and Storage, 4716 Hollywood Road, St. Joseph, Michigan 49085, 269-469-5049

Amanda Savage, Stratford Little Jelly Factory, 2 miles North of Stratford on Highway 77, Stratford, Oklahoma, 580-759-2093 (www.stratfordjelly.com)

James Shafer Farm, 721 W. Snow Road, Baroda, Michigan, 49101-9788, 269-422-1987

Shafer Orchards, 207 Shafer Road, Baroda, Michigan 49101 (www.parrett.net/~shafer/)

Dr. Bill Shane, Southwest Michigan Research and Extension Center, 1791 Hillandale Road, Benton Harbor, Michigan 49022 (www.maes.msu.edu/swmrec)

Edith Shilling

Jack Silver, Silver Mountain Vinegar, Austin, Texas 78709 (www.cantontradedays.com)

Sonrise Peach Farm, Gary Carter, 2¾ miles north or Stratford on the West Side Highway 77, Stratford, Oklahoma, 74872, 580-759-3787

South Carolina Peach Council and Staff

South Haven Memorial Library Staff, South Haven, Michigan

Cheri Taylor

R. James Taylor, Secretary of Trustees, Museum Director, Mary's City of David, Israelite House of David, 1903 as reorganized by Mary Purnell, 1930, Benton Harbor, Michigan 49023-0187 (www.marycityofdavid.org)

Linda Teale

Grace Topp

Barbara Totzke

Tree-Mendus Fruit, Inc., 9351 E Eureka Rd., Eau Claire, Michigan 49111 (www.treemendusfruit.com)

Gordon Twitchell

Vogel Orchards, 2 Miles West of Stonewall, Fredericksburg, Texas 78624, 830-644-2404 (www.vogelorchard.com)

David and Raulita Wade

Rev. William Wilson, Roseboom, New York

Margaret Whitmarsh

Brenda Black White

Bob Wooley, Coloma, MI

Delores Zunk, Hooker, Oklahoma

INDEX

Please send the following:

_____ copies of *Peaches & Past Times* @ $24.95 (U.S.) each	$_____
Postage and handling $4.00 for first book	$_____
Postage and handling $1.00 for each additional book	$_____
Texas residents $1.93 sales tax per book	$_____
TOTAL	$_____

MAIL TO:

P&P Publishing

3802 Antelope Trail

Temple, TX 76504

Check or Credit Card (U.S. funds only)

Charge to my ☐ Master Card ☐ Visa Card   expiration date _____

account# _____   signature _____

Name _____

Address _____

City _____ State _____ Zip _____

Phone _____ Email _____

ORDER ON LINE: www.pandppublishing.com

— —

Please send the following:

_____ copies of *Peaches & Past Times* @ $24.95 (U.S.) each	$_____
Postage and handling $4.00 for first book	$_____
Postage and handling $1.00 for each additional book	$_____
Texas residents $1.93 sales tax per book	$_____
TOTAL	$_____

MAIL TO:

P&P Publishing

3802 Antelope Trail

Temple, TX 76504

Check or Credit Card (U.S. funds only)

Charge to my ☐ Master Card ☐ Visa Card   expiration date _____

account# _____   signature _____

Name _____

Address _____

City _____ State _____ Zip _____

Phone _____ Email _____

ORDER ON LINE: www.pandppublishing.com